THE HARD TRUTH ABOUT SOFT SKILLS

Also by Peggy Klaus

BRAG! The Art of Tooting Your Own Horn Without Blowing It

THE HARD TRUTH ABOUT SOFT SKILLS

Workplace Lessons Smart People

Wish They'd Learned Sooner

PEGGY KLAUS

with JANE ROHMAN and MOLLY HAMAKER

Collins

An Imprint of HarperCollinsPublishers

The anecdotes in this book are drawn from real-life situations, but names and other identifying details have been changed.

HarperCollins books may be purchased for educational, business, or sales promotional use. For information, please write: Special Markets Department, HarperCollins Publishers, 10 East 53rd Street, New York, NY 10022.

FIRST EDITION

Designed by Joseph Rutt

Library of Congress Cataloging-in-Publication Data
Klaus, Peggy.
The Hard truth about soft skills : workplace lessons smart people
wish they'd learned sooner / Peggy Klaus. —1st ed.
p.   cm.
Includes index.
ISBN 978-0-06-128414-4
1. Communication in management. 2. Business communication.
3. Interpersonal relations. 4. Psychology, Industrial. I. Title.
HD30.3.K584 2007
650.1—dc22
2007023881

08 09 10 11 12   ID/RRD   11 10 9 8 7 6 5 4 3

To my clients,
whose enthusiasm for self-improvement
provides a constant source of inspiration.

CONTENTS

The impostor syndrome will follow you up the ladder.

A little humility takes you a long way.

THE HARD TRUTH ABOUT SOFT SKILLS

THE HARD TRUTH
ABOUT SOFT SKILLS

Why didn't someone tell me . . . and if they did, why didn't I listen?

This, as they used to say when I was growing up, is the $64,000 question. It's the one that comes up over and over again when the thousands of business professionals I coach and train each year tell me their tales from the trenches. Whether young or old, experienced or inexperienced, what strikes me most about their stories of missed opportunities and derailed careers is this: The source of their anxiety and frustration is rarely a shortfall in technical or professional expertise. Instead, it invariably stems from a shortcoming in their soft skills repertoire—the nontechnical traits and behaviors needed for successful career navigation.

But if these soft skills are really that important, why do so many people learn them the hard way? Because for the most part, people think soft skills don't really matter and are confused over exactly what they are.

IN SEARCH OF A DEFINITION

When it comes to soft skills, most people think they are all about those warm-and-fuzzy people skills. Yes, it's true people skills are a part of the equation, but that's just for starters. While hard skills refer to the technical ability and the factual knowledge needed to do the job, soft skills allow you to more effectively use your technical abilities and knowledge. Soft skills encompass personal, social, communication, and self-management behaviors. They cover a wide spectrum of abilities and traits: being self-aware, trustworthiness, conscientiousness, adaptability, critical thinking, attitude, initiative, empathy, confidence, integrity, self-control, organizational awareness, likability, influence, risk taking, problem solving, leadership, time management, and then some. Quite a mouthful, eh? These so-called soft skills complement the hard ones and are essential for success in the rough-and-tumble workplace. You can have all the technical expertise in the world, but if you can't sell your ideas, get along with others, or turn your work in on time, you'll be going nowhere fast.

NO RESPECT

However you define them, soft skills still suffer from a fundamental lack of respect. After all, how could anything described as soft be valued in the hard-charging, results-driven business world or impact the bottom line? Soft skills are generally viewed as "nice to have"—maybe even something you are just born with—but not critical for success. This attitude always makes me chuckle. It's like saying that Yo-Yo Ma has a brilliant career as a cellist solely because of his genes. While no doubt some of his musicianship and subsequent greatness may be linked to DNA, it belies all of the other elements that have contributed to his phenomenal success: disciplined study and practice, collaboration with ensembles, making sound career decisions, taking risks, developing and promoting his brand, dealing with conductors, and connecting with his audience. In Yo-Yo Ma's case, as in most situations, the soft skills are as important, if not more so, than the hard ones and deserve our respect. In other words, there's nothing *soft* about soft skills.

In fact, companies are finally starting to respect their value, linking competency in the soft skills arena to positive performance appraisals and salary increases. Soft skills have also become a significant consideration for firms in their recruitment efforts. A recent flurry of studies has underscored their value in the workplace, showing that soft skills competency can be as reliable an indicator of job performance as the more traditional qualifications of technical mastery or experience. One study found traits like conscientiousness and agreeability to be equally accurate predictors of work success as cognitive ability and work accuracy. Additional research, conducted with Fortune 500 CEOs by the Stanford Research Institute International and the Carnegie Mellon Foundation, found that 75 percent of long-term job success depends on people skills, while only 25 percent on technical knowledge. Another study of headhunters hiring CEOs ranked the ability to communicate and motivate as necessary attributes for positively affecting the bottom line.

Even though companies today are placing more value on soft skills, most of us are still out on our own when it comes to developing our personal repertoire. Despite collectively spending more than $50 billion on training programs for employees, many corporations fail to offer soft skills programs at all. And when they do provide them, the programs are often exclusively reserved for "high-potential" employees or senior executives. A comprehensive analysis of U.S. employer-sponsored training confirmed that the most frequently provided instruction consists of new employee orientation, computer applications for end users, technical skills or knowledge, and customer education. Soft skills training—which typically focused on communication and leadership—was provided "as needed," primarily for top executives. Unfortunately, college and university curriculums—even for advanced business degrees—are doing little more than the corporations when it comes to teaching soft skills. And it shows. A survey conducted by the Graduate Management Admission Council found that although MBAs were strong in analytical aptitude, quantitative expertise, and information-gathering ability, they were sorely lacking in other critical areas that employers find equally attractive: strategic thinking, written and oral communication, leadership, and adaptability. Increasing workplace and customer diversity across age, gender, racial, and ethnic lines—along with business globalization and virtual offices—have only heightened the need for strengthening soft skills competency.

HOW THIS BOOK WORKS

Throughout the years, I've collected stories about struggles and triumphs in the workplace based on thousands of hours training, coaching, and interviewing people at all levels on the corporate ladder. From these experiences, I've distilled fifty-four important workplace lessons that will increase your understanding and awareness of soft skills by showing you how they are woven throughout your career. Within these lessons, you'll also find practical insights, strategies, tools, and techniques for learning or improving a particular soft skills area. The lessons are organized into eight chapters, each covering particular aspects of your career in which soft skills play especially significant roles: career management, getting the job done, communication, handling critics, office politics, self-promotion, dealing with differences, and leadership.

In chapter 1, we'll dive into the most critical aspect of your career: managing it. Beginning with self-assessment and self-management, we'll explore a variety of soft skills topics, including lessons about decision making, risk taking, integrating work with your life goals, and maintaining high ethical standards.

Career survival depends on meeting your supervisor's agenda—not necessarily yours. In chapter 2, I shift the focus onto getting your job done. We'll cover the entire gamut of mission-critical soft skills lessons—from managing the details to managing your time, from being viewed as a problem solver with a can-do attitude to not letting the use of common sense fall through the cracks.

When it comes to communication, the whole shebang can do you in. That's why you need to be on high alert when it comes to everything from minding your words to minding your manners. And although technology has revolutionized communication, you'll find out in chapter 3 why the basics matter more than ever in a world that's filled with increasingly distracted people. I'll zero in on soft skills under the communication umbrella, such as opening your ears and adjusting your communication accordingly, asking the right questions, and displaying confidence and authenticity when presenting—even when your nerves are trying to get the best of you.

Chapter 4 brings you face-to-face with the realization that you are always being judged, so you better get used to it. From making a good impression the first time (and every time!) around to drawing on conflict-resolution techniques when confronted with heated situations, the lessons in this chapter will bring to life a variety of soft skills needed for handling criticism and your critics.

Are you apolitical and proud of it? Like the air we breathe, politics is everywhere, including at work. Yet when it comes to office politics, most people fall into three camps: those in denial, those who think they are above the fray, and those who claim playing politics at work simply isn't that important. Chapter 5 focuses on how misperceptions like these can send a career into the danger zone and why it's critically important to learn the un-spoken rules of your workplace. I'll highlight some of the essential soft skills of office politics: organizational awareness, spreading your influence, having a mentor, managing up, deflecting gossip, and handling office romance.

Chapter 6 starts off with a simple question: "Do you think branding is just for cows and that brag is a four-letter word?" If so, think again. In this chapter, I'll be covering some of the key soft skills associated with self-promotion, from personal branding so you stand out in the crowd to learning how to toot your own horn—especially when surrounded by people with sharp elbows.

As the forces of technology and globalization merge, our work-places are becoming increasingly diverse. The lessons in chapter 7 highlight the factors that can bring about friction, while offering a whole slew of soft skills for dealing with issues that rise from generational, gender, and cultural differences: emotional self-control, motivating those who operate from a different competitive mind-set, finding the best in every person, and keeping ourselves in check when it comes to stereotyping.

Do you have an assistant? Surprise! You're a manager. While for many the holy grail is a position in management, not every-one is cut out for the job—and those who do advance into man-agement roles often struggle with their leadership skills. From recognizing your strengths and weaknesses so you can address shortcomings to influencing people to think and act the way you want, in chapter 8 I'll uncover some of the most important soft skills just beneath the surface of good leadership. I'll end with some final thoughts on the benefits of having enough humility to know when it's time to go back to the drawing board.

So keep reading, and you'll find out more about how soft skills have a tremendous effect on nearly everything you need to do to get ahead at work. And *that's* the hard truth.

One

CONTROL YOURSELF

- Knowing yourself is as important as knowing how to do the job.

- There's no such thing as work-life balance, only trade-offs.

- Years of loyalty can work against you.

- Listen to your gut—it's full of data.

- No risks, no rewards.

- Get out of your own way.

- Learn the honest truth about integrity.

- You have to be good to be lucky.

A few years ago, an HR executive at a Fortune 500 company said to me, "Peggy, I can't believe how many people believe their bosses wake up in the morning thinking, 'Gee, let's see what I can do for *you* today.'" Her point was this: Chances are, nobody will ever care about your career more than you do—except for, well, maybe your parents or spouse. This means you must take responsibility for managing your own career—don't even think about leaving it to anyone else. I'm not saying that those around you at work aren't interested in helping you succeed. But their focus is mainly on themselves—their own projects, trajectory, and careers.

And similarly, your focus should remain squarely on you. Even when you don't work for yourself, managing your own career means wearing the many hats of an entrepreneur. Start thinking like the CEO, marketing manager, sales force, HR director, head of product design, and talent coordinator of your own company—a company of one, which is *you*.

Why is it so important that you take the reins when it comes to career management? First, gone are the days of job security. Mergers, acquisitions, downsizing, and international competition have done away with that. The average working American will now have between ten and twelve jobs and three to five careers during his or her lifetime. Second, people across the board—including your boss, his or her boss, and the HR director—are being asked to juggle more and more assignments, often combining the responsibilities of two or three people into one job. Most of the folks you assume are thinking about your career simply don't have the time or the energy, and you certainly can't expect them to be psychic when it comes to knowing what you want for your future. Third, those who let their careers "just happen" or expect employers to orchestrate them will end up disappointed. Unfortunately, most graduates are completely unprepared for their first encounter with these harsh realities—especially given that some of them have grown accustomed to e-mailing their college papers home for their parents to edit!

Whether just starting out or well on your way, one of the most important things you can do is take responsibility for yourself—your career, your goals, and your own behavior. Doing so begins with a very healthy dose of self-awareness and a commitment to self-management. Indeed, both are at the foundation of soft skills mastery—you'll see them time and time again throughout the rest of the book. In the lessons presented in this chapter, you'll find a variety of soft skills at play, including engaging in self-assessment on a continual basis, being personally accountable, creating a work life that makes sense, taking risks, listening to your intuition, and attracting luck. I'll also touch upon another soft skills area that will never go out of style: old-fashioned honesty and integrity.

KNOWING YOURSELF IS AS IMPORTANT AS KNOWING HOW TO DO THE JOB.

"Climb every mountain / Ford every stream / Follow every rainbow / Till you find your dream." Sound familiar? Sometimes when attending professional conferences, I feel like I am in a never-ending stage production of *The Sound of Music*. Motivational speakers shout from on high, "Follow your passion! If you think it, you will achieve it." I swear, if I hear one more person say something like that, I'm going off a Swiss alp. Which is probably why I relate so well to people who tell me how they wish they'd realized sooner that being passionate about something doesn't automatically mean you'll have the talent or aptitude to be successful at it. And even having all three—passion, talent, and aptitude—still doesn't guarantee success. One way of finding your bliss, your life's work, or simply something you won't mind spending eight to ten hours doing each day is to get to know yourself really, really well.

From my front-row seat, there's nothing soft about taking a hard look at who you are. After more than a decade of coaching people on all rungs of the career ladder, I find time and time again that the ones who have never taken an inventory of themselves wind up doing things that they aren't successful at or are miserable doing. They haven't thought enough about what kinds of tasks they like and dislike, which talents and interests they want to incorporate into their work life, or how their strengths and weaknesses might impact career choices. It's pretty simple, actually. Each of us has special gifts that are better suited to certain kinds of careers than others. If you seek out a line of work that's a good match, you'll more likely flourish. If you pursue an incompatible line of work, you'll more likely struggle. In order to learn where you'll thrive the most, take the time to get to know yourself better. Think of it as buying a special type of insurance that will make you less vulnerable to heartaches, anxiety, stress, and losing time or money.

That said, knowing what you are best suited doing workwise can be tricky. It's not always clear where your strengths lie from the start, so it can take some time and experience to figure it out. And sometimes we can learn the most from paying attention to our weaknesses. This was the case for thirty-eight-year-old Marta.

In the early years of her career, Marta changed jobs so often that it started to raise eyebrows and make potential employers think she was uncommitted, flighty, or someone who bored easily. In fact, her college friends nicknamed her "Froggy" from watching her leap from one job to another. But once she examined her strengths, she realized something very powerful about herself: she was what you could call a "fixer-upper"—not of old homes, but of businesses. As she explains, "I held a series of management positions at midsized firms. Each time I was hired, I was drawn into spending significant amounts of time finding ways to overhaul and improve the organization. As soon as things were running smoothly, I would become restless and move on to the next company and challenge." At first this pattern caused her to doubt her ability to stick with a position. The more she thought about it, however, the more she realized that her real passion and talent was not as a manager but as a business development specialist. So before her habit of switching jobs could become a career liability, she decided to launch her own consulting firm, which has since grown into a multimillion-dollar operation.

Whether just starting out or farther along the path, becoming and remaining successful is dependent not just on knowing who you are and what you are great at, but also on knowing how others think about you—even when the review is unfavorable. This means embracing your annual performance appraisal or 360-degree assessment (an approach that incorporates comprehensive feedback from everyone who interacts with you at work—colleagues, supervisors, team members, clients, and direct reports). Use these as an opportunity to think about your competencies and achievements, identify gaps, and make sure you are staying on track for doing what you want to do. Yes, what *you* want! Not what your parents, spouse, or bosses have in mind. Additionally, particularly in the early years of work or during a major transition, many people find meeting with a career counselor very helpful and clarifying.

THERE'S NO SUCH THING AS WORK-LIFE BALANCE, ONLY TRADE-OFFS.

"Peggy, for years I've juggled it all between my personal and professional life and I have just one thing to say about work-life balance: There's no such thing!" said Gabriella, the district manager for a major software development company. "I've had to come to terms with the fact that I can't be perfect or do it all, at least not all at the same time. Some days I'm a better sales manager than mother, other days a better spouse than a boss." She proceeded to explain that meshing work with life is an ongoing process of making choices and trade-offs, not some static state you achieve called balance.

I couldn't agree more. As Drew, one of my CEO clients, puts it, "If you keep adding new things to your plate, something that's already there is going to slide off." In his case, he was lamenting over what happened when his wife sent him to the grocery store over the weekend to pick up a few items. She had given him a list that instructed him to "buy a box of Danny's favorite cereal." Standing there in the aisle, scanning the rows of colorful boxes, he realized that he had absolutely no clue which one was his four-year-old's favorite. This got him wondering: When was the last times he had even been home when his son was eating breakfast? Which begged an even bigger question: Was this the life he wanted?

A major part of knowing yourself is making sure the career you create makes sense with the rest of your life. Just like you check the oil in your car, check in with yourself on a regular basis to keep tabs on how your trade-offs are affecting you. While it's true that certain personal characteristics remain constant, other aspects continue to evolve as we go. Oftentimes life intervenes and the objectives that once drove us, the values that influence our behavior, or our tolerance for risk change. What we were doing when we were younger may no longer suit us as we hit middle age. We get married or we get divorced. Children enter the picture and the circumstances in which we do our work matters more than the actual work we do. Or the business climate alters. The company gets sold. A new boss enters the picture. The firm or the economy hits a downturn. Or we simply become bored and restless from doing the same old thing. The ways in which our lives alter over time are endless. So that's why it's imperative to review on a regular basis your values, goals, and objectives to make sure that your work life and the rest of your life are still a good fit in terms of the trade-offs you are making.

One of my drama-school friends from England—a very good actor and director—is the perfect example of someone who was in desperate need of a work-life tune-up. After two decades in "the business," he was still earning a marginal income. He had to admit to himself that not only was he never going to become a star earning the big bucks, but there were no signs of him being able to support himself and his wife—and certainly not the children they were hoping to have someday—in the style he had imagined. It was then he realized that during the years, his greatest strength—his talent as an actor—had become his biggest liability by preventing him from having the life he wanted. So, yearning for a steadier paycheck, he put the word out that he was looking for a new line of work, something that would build off his creative strengths as a performer and as a "people person." Before long, he picked up a temporary assignment with a consulting company coaching business professionals on their presentation skills. Not only was he happily able to use many of his acting and directing skills, but the firm eventually hired him for a full-time position, which he has held for the last five years. And, just last summer, he asked for and was given six weeks off so he could direct a production of Shakespeare's *Twelfth Night* in Sweden. Finally, he's crafted a career for himself that he finds very rewarding on all levels.

So whenever your circumstances significantly change or you are feeling dissatisfied about work, do a "trade-off assessment" of how your career choices are impacting your overall life. Pay attention to gaps between the kind of life you want and the life you are actually living. If there are any big discrepancies, consider how to better align the two spheres and construct a career that makes more sense.

First and foremost, assess your employer's policies (flex time, part-time, etc.) and think about where you might be able to stretch them, like proposing a job share when there isn't already a program for that. In other words, don't rule things out just because the company or someone in your department has never done something before.

For instance, Lorraine, a fairly senior manager at a pharmaceutical company and mother of two young children, was going through a difficult divorce and had reached her wits' end. "I just can't do this anymore. I'm going to march right in there and resign," she announced to me.

"Whoa! " I said. "Sit down and don't do a thing until we hash this out."

With nearly full custody of the children, she really needed more time at home instead of traveling so much. Lorraine longed to walk her kids to school and meet them when they got off the bus, at least one day a week. For several months, she had been thinking about asking her boss if she could work from home on Fridays. But Lorraine was afraid to broach this, especially since she was worried about how the team of twenty people she manages—many with children themselves—would react.

"If you don't ask, you don't get. What's the very worst thing that could happen?" I asked her. Together, she and I role-played various scenarios, including possible responses from her boss. The next day she approached him. She said she felt like she was facing a firing squad.

Apparently, her fretting had been a total misfire. Her boss was incredibly understanding, "I didn't know you were going through all of this. Why didn't you mention it earlier? Of course you can take Fridays at home. Figure out how you can stay in touch with your group on that day and what you need to do to shore things up to make it work out as well as possible. In fact, if you need to work from home for two days for a while, then do that."

Sometimes we work ourselves up into such a dither that we box ourselves in and fail to see the possibilities. While Lorraine finally calmed down, she realized that when it comes to most things in life—including your career—everything's negotiable.

Start off by getting clear with yourself about what you want and what trade-offs you are willing to make and live with. For instance, are you willing to take a new job or lesser position within your existing company that you might not enjoy as much, but that offers a more flexible schedule? Can you afford earning a smaller salary for a job that better fits your current needs? Once you determine what will work best for you, strategize how to make it happen. Identify people who have been successful navigating through the company to get what they need and ask them for advice. Then go for it. Bottom line? While it's true that if you ask for something you *may* not get it, if you don't ask, you *definitely* won't get it!

YEARS OF LOYALTY CAN WORK AGAINST YOU.

In recent years, the revolving-door model of gaining job experience has taken root. I get whiplash just looking at Gen X and Y résumés and seeing how much they jump around. One thing's for sure: The number of years you stay with a company, which used to be a big selling point, is out the window. The world of hiring has been turned upside down. Now when HR looks at someone who has worked at the same place for ten years, all sorts of alarm bells go off—she can't be much of a risk taker; he's not cutting edge enough. Translation: old school. Dead weight. Dinosaur.

Today's organizations value people who are versatile. Presumably, if you've moved around from job to job—within reason, of course, and with good recommendations—you've been exposed to a wide range of situations and have demonstrated your ability to succeed in a business climate marked by constant change. Now, this doesn't mean that you need to start job-hopping or become a generalist. The key is to strike the right balance between taking on new positions and roles to increase your range of skills—which, by the way, can often be accomplished while working at the same company—and at the same time developing a reputation for being really good at something.

Don't wait like Sam did until it's too late. Sam had worked his way up in sales and marketing for one of the largest sporting goods manufacturers in the United States. Although he had been approached by competitors throughout the years, Sam loved the firm and had no intention of ever leaving. Then the company went through some major changes. Competition from lower-priced overseas manufacturers became fierce. The company was reorganized and downsized. During that period, Sam heard about an opening in another area of the firm and decided it was finally the time to stretch himself and try something different, even without a pay increase. He was completely shocked, however, when the higher-ups came back saying, "We really don't see you as having the skills for taking on this challenge." As Sam later found out, the company no longer had the luxury to risk putting someone in a position who might not succeed. He was about seven years too late. And then officials lowered the boom even more, announcing that while he could stay at the company, he would soon be demoted from his position as head of sales and marketing. They were bringing in a new leadership team with more e-tailing experience. In the end, Sam took early retirement.

If you want to stay competitive and ahead of the game, keep your hard skills sharp. Making this happen is not your employer's responsibility, it's yours. Benchmark your skills against your organization's competency profiles—the proficiencies and behaviors needed to succeed—for each level of your job. If your company's training or HR department doesn't provide these for you, get to know others in your field and find out what new skills they are tackling. Determine which of your own competency gaps are the most critical for success in your position and find ways to fill them, even if it means taking special courses on your own time using your own money. And if you can't develop your skills any further at your current job or position—think about finding a new one!

We're all familiar with the expression that the only constant is change. Although this thought can be traced all the way back to the Greek philosopher Heraclitus, it's never been truer than it is today. Change has become a mainstay of the workplace. While change can lead us to new opportunities, stimulate personal growth, and produce positive outcomes, we tend to resist it due to the difficulties and obstacles it brings in the short run. To successfully manage the transitions that will inevitably impact your life, remain flexible, bring your creativity, and embrace the journey of self-development. Success isn't a destination at which you finally arrive or a panoply of accumulated awards. Instead, it's a continual process that, like your career, continues until the day you retire.

LISTEN TO YOUR GUT—IT'S FULL OF DATA.

It's obvious that we should "think things over" before making decisions. But what about "feeling them over"? You know, checking in with your gut—or what some call intuition, which can be an important source of information during the decision-making process. How something sits with you is not just based on a tangle of emotions. Your gut contains a complete internal data bank full of valuable knowledge and experience.

Although you should pay attention to your gut, that doesn't necessarily mean you should follow exactly what it tells you! Although always informative, sometimes your gut feelings are irrational. For example, one of my colleagues was interviewing someone who was making him feel so uneasy that he didn't want to hire her. He couldn't figure out the source of his discomfort. She presented herself well, was articulate and personable, and had a terrific track record. By examining why his initial reaction was negative, he realized that her mannerisms reminded him of his older sister, with whom he had never gotten along. Did this prevent him from hiring the talented candidate? No. But he recognized the need to be careful about assuming she was going to be like his sister. By doing so, he was able to detach from his first impression and go on to form a positive relationship with the new hire on the basis of her actual performance.

Conversely, we've all heard "something didn't feel quite right" stories in which trusting one's gut saved the day. Gregory, a financial manager, had such an experience. Reviewing plans for a major business acquisition, he had the sense that something didn't sit quite right, even though everyone else involved was ready to say yes to the deal. While he couldn't put his finger on it, he kept feeling something was amiss and went over everything one more time, spending most of a weekend combing the paperwork. Sure enough, there it was, buried deep inside a report—a miscalculation that everyone had missed. The proposal seemed too good to be true because it was. Exploring his gut reaction saved the company from making a big mistake to the tune of $3 million!

Listening to your gut can give you invaluable insights if you approach it in a measured way. Next time your gut is calling, do the following:

- Observe what you are feeling.

- Put the feelings in words.

- Ask yourself whether your feelings are based on a legitimate or an irrational interpretation of the situation.

- If the answer is that the feelings are based on an irrational interpretation or assumption on your part, then recognize where they are coming from—as did my colleague above who realized the job candidate reminded him of his sister—and move on without letting yourself be unreasonably influenced by those feelings.

- If you think that your feelings are based on legitimate concerns, then explore them further before moving forward.

- Before sharing your gut feelings with others, make sure you can support them with a thoughtfully reasoned-out position.

NO RISKS, NO REWARDS.

Bill, a senior attorney whom I was coaching through a difficult transition, like so many seasoned professionals I've encountered, was learning a lesson long past due: to get what he wanted, he was going to have to step out of his comfort zone and take some risks. After years of making personal sacrifices for work, Bill was coming to grips with the realization that he would probably never make partner. As we discussed his next move, he paused and said to me, "I've never gotten used to worrying about billable hours and the stress of working ninety hours a week. I've never really admitted this before, but the truth is I wish I could just teach law. When I've taken on the occasional night course, I loved being around the students and the academic environment." Hallelujah, the truth comes out. Let's hope it sets Bill free.

So what's *your* tolerance for risk? Earlier in this chapter, I talked about how change is not only desirable but inevitable, whether welcomed or not. Even if you are happily humming along in your own little world, you aren't exempt. Like an unexpected guest, change will encroach. Your company merges or goes under. A new boss comes on the scene. There's a reorganization and you're given different responsibilities. Amid it all, one thing's for certain. Change will force you to make choices that involve varying degrees of risk. So ask yourself this: How you are going to deal with risk when it comes knocking at your door? Will you run and hide or embrace it with open arms? The best way to prepare for risk is to become aware of your comfort level with it in general.

Those who are risk averse like the comfort and security of doing the same things over and over again. There's really nothing wrong with that unless it stops you from making improvements to a less-than-optimal situation. I've known people who are truly unhappy with their jobs, but sit around complaining for years on end instead of doing something to change the situation. And it's often due to an aversion to taking risk or trying something new, as was the case for Bill, the attorney at the beginning of this section.

Don't get me wrong here. I'm not asking you to engage in what's called risky behavior, which refers to doing things that are impulsive or even dangerous. Some people are too impulsive and need to be more cautious. That was the case with Charlie. The founder and executive director of a large nonprofit, he was temporarily lured away by a lucrative job with an up-and-coming consulting firm. Burned out after years of fighting with state bureaucrats for funds, at the height of the dot-com boom Charlie jumped at the chance of returning to the corporate world and becoming a high-paid consultant. He was so excited that he took a three-month leave of absence and rented an office near his home, figuring that he could ease into the new position and start consulting with clients while running the search for his permanent replacement at the nonprofit. Ten weeks into the arrangement, Charlie realized he had made a huge mistake. He hated not running his own show and he didn't like working solo, without the hum of an office buzzing around him. Furthermore, traveling and being away from his family for four and five days at a time made him depressed. Suddenly, the nonprofit job was looking a whole lot better than it had a few months ago when he had jumped into the new position.

As Charlie's story suggests, avoiding risk isn't necessarily a bad habit that you need to stop, nor is being risk friendly automatically a good quality. What everyone does need to do, however, is to become more self-aware about his own level of risk tolerance so he is better prepared for change. For example, another client who worked in corporate America, Clarissa, came to me feeling like her job wasn't the best fit for her freethinking spirit. She was considering starting her own business. I asked her to conduct a risk assessment using the following:

- Assess your level of comfort with risk in general.

- Identify the pros and cons of the particular risk.

- Consider what your gut is telling you and determine whether it's a valid concern that requires more investigating.

- If you decide to take the risk, develop a strategy for sustaining yourself during the transition. Having a strategy helps risk-averse people feel less anxious and encourages risk-friendly types to be more methodical about their decision in order to avoid impulsivity.

- Once you've made the decision to take a risk, line up the people and resources you'll need to be successful.

- Prepare some "what if" alternatives in case your plans don't work out.

Clarissa came back admitting that while she wanted to be an entrepreneur, she was unwilling to forgo having a steady income at the present time. Although it was going to take $75,000 to launch the business, she decided that $25,000 was the most she felt comfortable borrowing. Given all of this data, she decided to keep her current job and start her business on the side, or as she said, "put my toes in the water, then jump in if everything works out." After two years, the new business was doing great and it was time to make the plunge. She quit her job and became a full-time entrepreneur.

Risk taking isn't just about deciding whether to leap from one job or career to the next. It shows up throughout our work lives. For example, Phillip, an executive for a clothing manufacturer, was afraid of giving his opinions in meetings. More often than not, the division head was condescending and dismissive about anyone's input. Ironically, this company had just spent millions of dollars trying to change its corporate culture into a kinder, gentler, more communicative one. Believe me, the irony of this was not lost on anyone attending those meetings. So, fearful of being put down in front of the group, Phillip continued to retreat. As he remarked in a coaching session, "Peggy, I'm not willing to speak up and be knocked down or humiliated." But there was a big problem with Phillip's approach. By not speaking up, his leadership skills had become invisible. I pointed out to him that he was stuck in "either-or" thinking—that is, he would either be shut up or shot down. Instead, he needed to be proactive and anticipate Mr. Dismissive's remarks ahead of time. I suggested to Phillip that he preface his comments at the meeting with something along these lines: "I know this is a difficult subject, but I would be doing you and the group a disservice if I didn't bring this up." Or "In light of what we've all been learning in our training about valuing everyone's input, here are my own thoughts on how to approach the issue." After that, if Mr. Dismissive still had the audacity to shoot down the input, he would be the only humiliated person in the room.

GET OUT OF YOUR OWN WAY.

Last fall I called a senior Wall Street investment banker at home on a weekend. During the time I had worked with her, we became good friends and I had gotten to know her family as a result. So when her nine-year-old son answered the phone, I asked him how things were going at school. He hemmed and hawed, then finally told me that he was disappointed with himself for backing out of running for student council at his school, which was attended by students from kindergarten through sixth grade. I asked him why he didn't run, and he answered, "I didn't think they would ever pick a fourth grader." But it turned out they had. The only two classmates who had applied, Malcolm and Emma, were also in the fourth grade, and they had both been asked to serve. In the background, I heard his mother say with exasperation, "Peggy, I told him just like I tell my group at work: You need to stop making excuses and get out of your own way." Funny how from fourth-grade student council to the grown-up corporate world, some habits die hard. Her comment took me right back to countless situations I've observed over the years, including a facilitation session that I led with members of her team a year ago.

Me to junior banker: So, what would you like your boss [seated in room] to do?

Junior banker turning to his boss: Jackie, I would like you to think of me as a senior banker.

Me to junior banker: I need you to be specific here so I can understand what you mean by that.

Junior banker: Um-m-m, I want her to respect me as a peer.

Me to junior banker: Yes, but what does that mean? What would it look like if she did respect you as a peer?

Junior banker (growing more frustrated): Well, I think she should think of me when new business comes to our group.

Me to junior banker: I don't know what you mean when you say you want her to think of you for new business. Please tell her exactly what you want her to do.

Junior banker, nearly at wits' end, turns to his boss and blurts out: I want you to give me five of your biggest accounts.

Me to junior banker and Jackie: All right, now I understand what you want. Jackie, do you understand as well?

Jackie to junior banker: Look, I'm more than happy to give you five of my largest accounts, which is what I told you six months ago. In fact, we made an agreement that you would first accomplish four things that I would hold you accountable for doing. But you haven't done a single one and you keep saying it's because you are too busy with this or that. So, tell me, why should I think of you as a senior banker and turn over five important clients when you've acted like that?

Me to junior banker: Is this what happened?

Junior banker (shrinking about three inches lower into his padded leather chair): Um-m-m, yes.

Next time you feel stuck, take a good hard look at yourself and what's really keeping you from getting what you want. Chances are, no one is in the way but you.

LEARN THE HONEST TRUTH ABOUT INTEGRITY.

"I didn't think it was wrong using the extra points generated by my boss's corporate credit card to buy electronics for myself. Even though he knew about the points, they just sat there unused year after year. If someone didn't redeem them soon, they were going to expire," said Howard, a thirtysomething administrative assistant. His boss had recently discovered the shopping spree and now Howard was looking for a new job.

Let me cut right to the ethical chase. If you find yourself having to defend yourself and make an argument for why your behavior really is okay, then you've probably crossed what I call the IC Divide—the IC here stands for integrity and character. And once you've crossed it, it's extremely hard to backpedal into the realm of good grace again.

I recently read a disturbing statistic. More than 50 percent of college graduates admitted to lying on their résumés. Not so long ago, I was asked to appear on a national morning show to discuss cheating at work in the wake of a highly successful dean of a prestigious university lying about her college degree. If you can believe it, she didn't have one.

In a preinterview, the show's producer asked me, "When is it okay?"

"Okay to do what?" I asked.

"To lie about your credentials," she responded.

"Never. In my book lying and cheating are never okay."

There are no gray areas when it comes to Howard stealing

credit card points or the college dean, as one newspaper euphemistically called it, "padding her resume." You never claim credit for what you haven't earned or take what isn't yours. And yes, that includes office supplies!

A friend of mine was assisting her boss, the owner of a small consulting company, during a program he was giving at an accounting firm. The consultant was told to store his things in the conference room cabinet, which was stocked full of office supplies.

"He didn't see me, but I saw him stuff his briefcase with Post-it notes, pens, and boxes of staples. I couldn't believe it!"

A few weeks later, my friend resigned from her position. Her boss's seemingly minor infraction, along with some other slightly questionable behavior, spoke volumes about his character and integrity. If he felt fine about ripping off his longtime client, maybe he would feel just as fine ripping off an employee.

Even if you think you can get away with cheating, lying, or stealing, your actions are bound to catch up with you sooner or later. The plethora of newspaper articles on corporate scandals underscore that truth. And these days, with the Internet, sources and facts are only a click away.

The old platitude "Your reputation is everything" is even truer now than when your parents were climbing up the ladder. In today's virtual world, reputation is not only everything, but everywhere. When you cross the IC Divide, you risk damning yourself in cyberspace for all of eternity.

If you're not careful in our virtual world, it's also easy to inadvertently raise eyebrows—without even knowing it. Jim, a recent college graduate looking for a job in the mortgage industry, noted, "If someone Googles my name, the first thing that pops up is a picture of me dressed in a toga partying it up. Somehow that picture made its way into my fraternity's national online newsletter. Believe me, it's not exactly the image I want to be portraying to a potential employer." Unfortunately, there's not much Jim can do to make that image go away—and I'm not saying you should stop going to parties. But just imagine if what had popped up on Google instead was a blog entry of Jim dissing his last employer.

The key to keeping yourself out of hot water is to create a personal code of conduct, then stick to it. Know your company's values, not just the rules and regulations. Weigh your actions against both personal and company principles, then hold yourself to the highest standards. Act in the spirit of the law, not just to meet the lowest standards set for you.

Last, but not least, if you find that you're whispering the following kinds of statements to yourself, think long and hard about what you're *really* doing:

- It won't matter just this once.

- They'll never miss it.

- Well, I didn't break any laws.

- It's not such a big deal.

- Aren't rules made to be broken?

YOU HAVE TO BE GOOD TO BE LUCKY.

One morning when my husband and I were vacationing in Italy with friends, we met up with another group of American travelers over breakfast. One of my friends struck up a conversation with a member of the other group, a professor of business at a major university in Southern California. He asked her what she did for work, and she explained that she was an organizational development consultant with her own firm. He then asked where she had gotten her MBA. She told him that she didn't have one—in fact, her only college degree was a BA in psychology. "I started out in the nonprofit world, where I held senior management positions," she explained. "After my children were born, I wanted something more flexible and kind of fell into project consulting. Over the years, one thing led to another and now my little serendipitous enterprise is sending those kids to college!" He gave her an incredulous look, then told her that he found her story quite remarkable, especially since many of his colleagues with PhDs in business were chomping at the bit to start consulting practices. Yet not one of them had ever been able to get a company off the ground. "I guess you were incredibly lucky," he concluded.

"One of the great fallacies about success is that we somehow stumble upon it through luck. I hate it when people look at what I've accomplished and tell me how lucky I've been. Luck has nothing to do with it," said Betsy, a brilliant advertising executive who runs her own midwestern agency, after I told her my Italy story. "Please set things straight in your book about the role of luck in one's career," she begged me. "Maybe when it comes to winning the lottery luck calls the shots, but nine times out of ten in business, success comes from having the right attitude—not from magical influences that are out of your control." I couldn't agree with Betsy more. Getting what's called "a lucky break" is almost always the result of groundwork we ourselves laid. While success unquestionably requires hard work, self-awareness, and aptitude, equally important are what I call the "make your own luck" factors: being open to reaching out to others and new ideas, listening to your gut, believing you will succeed, being able to shift your game plan or priorities, and knowing how to turn lemons into lemonade—things that are harder to quantify and are more attitudinally based.

You can't court luck with wishful thinking alone. Or as Betsy puts it, you have to be good to be lucky. Fortunately, with a little effort, anyone can cultivate the habits that will bring more luck into their lives. If you have your nose to the grindstone but are still not quite getting there, then maybe it's time to make more luck for yourself. You can start by asking yourself these questions:

- Do you stick to the routine at work or make a point of gaining new skills, taking on special projects, and learning about different aspects of the company?

- How did you respond the last time something went wrong? Were you able to convert the challenge into an opportunity?

- When was the last time you listened to your intuition or gut feelings and the last time you didn't? What were the outcomes in each situation?

- When you encounter interesting new people, do you make a genuine connection with them and go to the effort to stay in touch?

- Are you absolutely convinced that you are going to succeed? Do you expect positive things to happen to you? If not, why not?

Remember, there's nothing dumb about luck.

Two

GETTING THE JOB DONE

- Your boss wants *you* to figure it out.

- Learn when to stick and when to shift or the details will hang you.

- When you can't deliver, don't say yes . . . but be careful how you say no.

- Your procrastination is trying to tell you something.

- Whining is for kids . . . and even then, no one wants to hear it.

- Manage your meetings . . . or else.

- Common sense is far too uncommon.

Given that it makes me a member of what's sometimes called America's most self-absorbed generation, I sometimes hate to admit to being a baby boomer. Fortunately, though, being self-absorbed is not entirely a bad thing. As with most other aspects of life, it's all a matter of degree and circumstance. In chapter 1, I pointed out that you *do* need to be thinking of yourself when it comes to making career choices because no one else is going to be doing that for you. On the other hand, when it comes to actually getting your job done, it's time to shift the focus off of you and on to "them"—your boss and his or her boss, your coworkers, people in other departments, clients, customers, and the organization at large. When doing the job, your survival and success will depend largely on collaboration on a variety of fronts and on meeting agendas set by other people. Having a service orientation toward others is a soft skill in itself.

If you fail to make this critical shift in gears from you to them, most likely you'll be setting yourself up for unrealistic expectations and you'll irritate your coworkers. This is the case with many folks who are just entering the workforce. You know you are in trouble if you expect to be promoted to CEO of a major Fortune 500 company by the time you are thirty or think the baby boomers should take early retirement so you can move into their positions sooner. If you find yourself thinking along these lines and can't come to grips with readjusting your expectations, then you'll probably do best starting your own company. That's because I can tell you this right now: Few boomers are going to accelerate their plans for retirement so that Max or Madison with little experience can move into their hard-won positions.

In this chapter, you'll see in action a wide variety of must-have soft skills for doing your work, including taking the initiative, knowing how to handle the details, managing your workload, improving your time-management skills, possessing the right attitude, problem solving, and using one of the best soft skills of all: common sense.

YOUR BOSS WANTS *YOU* TO FIGURE IT OUT.

Imagine this: You're a hardworking assistant tucked away in some backwater sales office far away from corporate headquarters. You've been thinking that the company is missing a big opportunity with a certain market sector. After doing some Internet research, you become even more convinced and dash off an analysis of your idea, including its relevance for the company. You sheepishly send it to your boss, expecting it to get lost in his overflowing inbox, but before you know it, your e-mail has been forwarded to the biggies at corporate headquarters on the other side of the country, who are now reading it and passing it among themselves. Next thing you know, you receive a personal note from the VP of sales and marketing for the entire firm, complimenting your great work and saying that your idea will be discussed at the upcoming meetings for revising the company's marketing plan.

Irene, now the head of sales and marketing for a major specialty foods company, was that hardworking assistant. By taking the initiative, she overturned the "surely-someone-knows-more-about-this-than-me" myth. Calling it one of the most pivotal lightbulb moments in her career, Irene said, "It's only natural to think that the people above us have all the answers or even the right questions. But a lot of the time, they don't! Maybe it's because they lack the time to pursue a need, or they are simply too busy to identify an issue in the first place. Whatever the case, if you notice something, don't wait for someone to ask you to address it."

I can already hear the "buts," as in:

But this won't fly with the people I work with—they're really smart and have been in the business a long time. I'm sure they've already thought of everything.

Wrong! They haven't. Trust me.

But the bosses will feel threatened.

Yes, some might. But don't forget, they also want to look good in front of their own boss. Your success reflects well on their management abilities—it means they have trained you well.

But it's too risky sticking my neck out. My little take-initiative project could make me the laughingstock.

It's true, your idea may be rejected. But I bet you anything people are going to remember your name, just because you were able to think outside the box.

Do you want to argue with me or do you want to put the "buts" aside and take the initiative? Think about Irene before you decide.

LEARN WHEN TO STICK AND WHEN TO SHIFT OR THE DETAILS WILL HANG YOU.

When it comes to getting the job done, your attention to detail can end up being a blessing or a curse.

On the one hand, not focusing on the details enough will get you into hot water; on the other hand, focusing on details too much can prove paralyzing. The first scenario is exactly what happened to me years ago during my first job in television as a talent coordinator for a comedy show. This is when I first learned the lesson "always consider the 'what ifs.'" After making it through the season's first four shows without any significant problems, I approached the fifth show with no worries. Of the six comics scheduled to appear, two had already arrived the night before from New York, one lived within driving distance of our studio in Northern California, and the remaining three were on a one-hour flight from Los Angeles that was scheduled to arrive in San Francisco ninety minutes before start time. Everything seemed under control. But an hour before we were scheduled to tape in front of a live studio audience with a union crew (translation: major dollars being expended every minute), I got word that the San Francisco airport was completely fogged in. This meant that the plane carrying the three comics from Los Angeles couldn't land. It was now headed for San Jose, an hour's drive from our studio. I completely panicked. In fact, I was hyperventilating. Union rules and the money situation dictated that we begin without them. I cursed myself for not thinking about the "what ifs" before the fog rolled in. Come to think of it, why hadn't someone told me to do that? Fortunately, my producer—who managed to keep his composure—said to me, "Peggy, next time make sure to get them on an earlier flight to give us some wiggle room." You better believe that for the sixth show I scheduled the performers to come in the night before, and if they couldn't, at least three hours in advance with backup plans from other airports. Ever since that night, I've paid more attention to the details—especially the things that can go wrong—and always run through in my mind what I now call the "what ifs"?

On the flip side, people with perfectionist tendencies sometimes need to let go of the details. This was Jared's experience. A self-confessed detail lover, he often got so hung up on the details that he lost sight of the big picture—the one that senior management was hoping he would see. His hyperfocus was also driving his staff crazy. With the best of intentions, Jared wanted to make sure that each situation was handled correctly. But as a result, he meddled where he shouldn't have so often that his staff found themselves in the impossible position of being afraid to make a move without him. But if they asked for his input, they knew it was likely to delay the project even further, to the point of missing deadlines and sales opportunities.

In this information-overload environment in which we operate today, getting mired in the details is a growing problem. Yet at the same time, we are asked to make business decisions at the speed of light. As one professional wrote to me, when it comes to the details, you need to learn when to stick and when to shift, a phrase she often repeats to herself:

Stick and shift.
Stick and shift.
Stick and shift.

People who tend to be underfocused on details need to stick on them longer. People who are hyperfocused on the details need to shift off and move on. Most of us fit somewhere in between and need to become fluent in knowing when to stick and when to shift. Otherwise, you might just find yourself spinning your wheels and going nowhere fast.

WHEN YOU CAN'T DELIVER, DON'T SAY YES . . . BUT BE CAREFUL HOW YOU SAY NO.

Whether helping out on a key assignment or serving on a special committee, it's tempting to take on extra work when someone you want to please—especially your boss—asks you to help out. Sometimes we say yes to avoid losing an anticipated promotion or raise and other times because we are flattered to be needed. But despite even the best of intentions, saying yes often backfires big time once we realize that we are lacking the time and resources to get it done right, we can't deliver as promised, or that we really don't want to do what we've agreed to. That's when a combination of fear and resentment sets in, making us wonder why we ever said yes in the first place. Being able to manage your workload includes learning to handle the "extras" that your boss and others attempt to add to your plate. And the key to doing this well comes from mastering the art of knowing when and how to say no.

"We all have to make sacrifices early on to establish a sense of dependability, but after you've done that, you really have to pick and choose," said Todd, a single father of two and head of operations for an electronics company. He added, "We're all stretched to the max, but a sustained diet of taking on more than you can handle is a sure recipe for disappointment." That was the case for

Vickie. When asked to serve on the board at her local country club where many of the higher-ups from her firm also belong, she saw it as an amazing networking and career-advancing opportunity. "Between everything going on at work and Little League with the kids, I completely spaced out on attending the first meeting. And then to my horror, I did the same thing with the next one! Now I'm so embarrassed. Your name becomes mud when you commit to something and then don't follow through. That's so much worse than just saying you can't do it in the first place—everyone hates a no-show."

"Just as important as saying no when you need to is the manner in which you say it," said Faye, a thirty-five-year-old financial planner who runs a sizable department. "The last thing you want to do is to come off like you're being difficult, uncooperative, or a prima donna." For example, if your boss asks you to join a company steering committee she's on, don't say no outright. Ask her to help you prioritize.

For example, avoid saying . . .

No, I'm sorry, I just can't. You've already given me too much work as it is!

Instead, say . . .

I would love to, but if I take this on, I'll need to postpone one of the three other projects you've recently given me. Which of them would you like me to put on hold so I can join the committee?

Or . . .

I'm so sorry, but I better pass on this one. If I add another assignment right now, I won't be able to give my best to everything else that I'm already working on. Please ask me again another time and perhaps I can help out then.

Next time before your lips say, "Sure, I can get this to you by Friday," when your head is telling you, "No way can I deliver it by then," strategize how to turn your boss down in a way that will earn you respect.

YOUR PROCRASTINATION IS TRYING TO TELL YOU SOMETHING.

Procrastination typically gets a bad rap. It's become synonymous with avoidance behavior and being lazy, irresponsible, or a goof-off. But sometimes your procrastination is trying to tell you something, and not paying attention to it can create big problems. So what might it be saying? Listen carefully. You might be surprised.

Florence, a freelance business magazine writer, is always under deadline and found herself in a continual state of panic from being behind schedule. When we started dissecting her approach to tackling assignments from start to finish, she recognized something about herself for the first time. "As much as I try, the process can't be rushed. I can't go straight to the computer and start writing. I need time to let things simmer first, usually as I go through the day—running errands, driving the kids to school, or even while mowing the lawn. This is how I best absorb and distill information about the topic and tease out how I want to work the piece. I can't skip this stage." In Florence's case, her procrastination was telling her to slow down at the beginning so she could mull things over more. Unfortunately, she hadn't been factoring in enough time for this to happen, which was leaving her feeling rushed and frantic. When planning her schedule, she needed to budget time for her thoughts to marinate. What she had been thinking of as procrastination was a significant part of her creative process. So when planning your own schedule—or when other people are putting you under deadline—be sure to allow enough preparation and percolation time.

Your procrastination holds all sorts of other surprises. What else could it be telling you? Here are a few more possibilities.

You don't have everything you need to get the job done. People put things off when they don't have the facts, finances, manpower, or some combination thereof to get the job done. Instead of recognizing this early on and going back to take care of critical gaps from the get-go, they plow ahead. As deadlines loom, the situation only worsens. Now they're really under pressure to move ahead with half a deck in half the time. They could have saved themselves enormous stress and worry by identifying the shortcomings in the beginning, then taken time—when they still had plenty of it—to address the problem. Waiting until they're under the gun puts them in a compromising position. Either they can go ahead and do the job, but not nearly as well as they should have, or start making excuses about why they're not going to make the deadline. The boss doesn't want an e-mail twenty-four hours before the due date asking for more information or resources. And pointing fingers or blaming is ineffective at best and childish at worst. Deadline disasters are easily avoided by taking the time up front to fill the holes.

You need to improve your time-management skills. Making promises we can't keep, like missing deadlines or being a no-show at meetings, is the kiss of death in any workplace. And it takes some serious effort to always meet our obligations. But while some people seem to come out of the womb with their day planners in hand, the rest of us learn this the hard way. One of the most important first steps in improving your time-management skills is to get organized. The number one way to do that is by having a good calendar system that works for you—either on your computer, on your PDA, or on paper, the old-fashioned way. It doesn't matter which, just make sure that you pick something you can religiously stick to. Second, if you are truly disorganized by nature, a competent assistant is invaluable. If you don't have the type of job that includes an assistant, these days your electronic devices, project-planning software, and online services can be set up to send reminders for appointments and otherwise act as a virtual assistant. Third, as I mentioned earlier, make sure not to underestimate the amount of time that things will take. Being an optimist is a wonderful quality, but it has its limits. In this instance, it can do you in. Leave yourself some wiggle room for the "what ifs." How much wiggle room you need is a judgment call based on time constraints, knowing yourself, understanding your work environment, and how much you are depending on others. Indeed, a good rule of thumb is that the more people involved, the more slack you should allow. Of course, if it's just you, maybe you're so pitifully understaffed that not even a miracle would get the project finished on schedule! Probably one of the biggest ways you can improve your time-management practice is my fourth and last point. Chunk it out. Sometimes people don't plan well because they guesstimate based on the entire project rather than breaking things down into smaller pieces, then setting time frames and schedules for each part. The more you break the project down into manageable chunks, the more accurate your scheduling will become.

It's time for a change. Do you have the resources you need to get the job done? Are you already on top of your time-management game? If the answer to both is yes, and you're still finding it hard to do the work, then your procrastination might be telling you that you are feeling bored or unchallenged and it's time to try something new. Find ways to get out of your rut by first considering opportunities within your current position, company, and career. Then look elsewhere, if necessary. Nothing fuels procrastination more than losing your enthusiasm.

WHINING IS FOR KIDS . . .
AND EVEN THEN, NO ONE WANTS TO HEAR IT.

No one likes a whiny kid, but a whiny grown-up is intolerable. Even though they should know better, some people just can't stop themselves: "We've tried this before and it's not going to work." Or "What makes you think it's going to be any different this time around?" Or "The coffee here is always too strong. How does anyone expect me to drink this crap?"

Barbara, a highly successful real estate agent in Los Angeles, explained that one of the most valuable gifts she ever received was when her friends performed a "whining intervention" on her. "Over dinner one night, a couple of my closest friends point-blank told me that they couldn't stand to be around me anymore because of my constant complaining about a problem I was having with the management of the realty firm I work for," she said. Her friends gave her an ultimatum: either shut up or take some action to solve the problem. So what did Barbara do to snap herself out of whining mode? First, she identified specific steps to improve her situation. For example, Barbara met with the president of the firm to share her concerns and to suggest some solutions. Not only did he listen, but he praised her for being a problem solver and agreed immediately to implement one of her suggestions, which was to put together a staff meeting to solicit ideas of what the company could be doing better. "It sounds so darn simple," Barbara said, "but I wish someone had told me a lot sooner to dump my 'poor me, the sky is falling' attitude."

Barbara had learned the key characteristic of problem solvers everywhere: knowing how to adjust your attitude. Just a simple turn can make all the difference. Take Suzanne, for example. After her smaller prestigious bank was swallowed up by a larger institution ten times its size, she walked around like a kid who didn't get the toy she wanted for Christmas. Suzanne whined to anyone and everyone about how the bank was now going to be too big and would lose all the intimacy that made it so great to work for. She lamented how the new firm didn't have the reputation and expertise that the old one did. As the weeks wore on, her venting became a major annoyance to her colleagues. In fact, Suzanne's teammates had started to keep their distance to avoid listening to her tirades. For Suzanne's boss, this period of mourning had gone on long enough. He pulled me aside one day while I was doing some other coaching work at the firm and said, "Peggy, you've got to talk to Suzanne. Before the merger, I had been planning to promote her. But right now, given all her whining, I'm much more inclined to fire her instead."

Later that day, I found a few minutes to meet with Suzanne and told her the following:

- The acquisition is a done deal.

- You *must* get over it *now*.

- If you can't get over it, get out. Otherwise, you may be asked to go.

- If you decide to stay, adopt a new attitude.

I suggested that she start by making a list of things that improved as a result of the acquisition. From what I had heard others in the bank saying, the change wasn't all bad by a long shot.

So that's what Suzanne did, and in the process she decided that she wanted to stay. Once she stopped whining, she realized that she needed to acquaint herself with the new people from the "other" bank and ask how she could be of help to them. About two months later, I ran into Suzanne again. She excitedly told me that she had been asked to sit on the high-profile transition committee that reported directly to the new CEO of the company. And, yes, about a year later, Suzanne was promoted.

Let's face it, life is unpredictable. As much as we try to plan for and control outcomes, nothing is ever a sure bet. So one of your best defenses against the unpredictable is developing an attitude that will best serve you and those around you. While you can't always control what's going to happen to you, you can control how you react and respond to the ups and downs. Indeed, how you deal with not getting what you want—just think of the poor impression conveyed when you witness a sore loser—speaks volumes in itself. When faced with difficulties and challenges, cultivating a constructive attitude to make things work is always the goal. Does that mean that you can't express disappointment? Of course not! But do it gracefully and appropriately, then move on and get over it—the quicker the better. A positive attitude sets the tone for not only yourself, but for everyone around you as well.

I know. You might be wondering whether it's possible for certain people to develop a more constructive attitude. As one woman remarked, "My boss is the most ornery person in the world. She's had a rough life. I don't think anything or anyone will ever reverse that." No matter how complicated, arduous, or disappointing our lives, we decide each and every moment of the day whether to see the glass as half empty or half full. So if you're in need of an attitude adjustment or overhaul, work on the following:

- Realize that a positive attitude is one of the most valuable assets you can possess. It creates far-reaching ripples both internally and externally, affecting everything around you.

- Always be on your best behavior—even when life throws you zingers.

- Smile more. It's amazing how much an increase in smiling changes everyone's mood for the better.

- Resist feeding negativity with complaining, blaming, and gossiping.

- A bad attitude often comes from feelings of impotency or helplessness. You can improve your attitude immeasurably by putting together an action plan for moving past these feelings.

MANAGE YOUR MEETINGS . . . OR ELSE.

"My mom talks on the phone, works on her computer, and goes to meetings all day." That's how a ten-year-old schoolmate of the daughter of my client Anna described what her mother does for a living. "I was driving the girls home from an outing when she told me that. I laughed and said it sounds like her mom and I do the same thing," Anna explained to me. "Although I found out later that we were in completely different lines of work, each of us was spending a vast majority of our time stuck in meetings."

Anna and the schoolmate's mother—like, well, every other adult I know in a white-collar job in corporate America today— are struggling with meeting madness. Many professionals feel overwhelmed and overscheduled with nonstop meetings that seem to prevent them from actually getting any real work done except before 5:00 a.m. and after 5:00 p.m. One high-level executive was beside herself when a woman had the nerve to follow her into the bathroom during a meeting break in an attempt to continue asking her questions. At least the guys in attendance couldn't follow suit!

Yet meetings don't always deserve the bad rap that they typically get, and indeed many can be invaluable. For example, a planning meeting—even a very long one—can save weeks of struggle if everyone walks away with clarity and direction so that nobody comes back three months later saying, "Well, I didn't know *that's* what you meant." Even if most meetings are not as valuable as they could be, you better get used to meetings, because they are definitely here to stay. As the economy has become increasingly competitive and businesses have become more complicated, the advantages of working collaboratively have proven themselves. This means that employees are likely to end up in even more meetings—be it those that are scheduled or unscheduled, formal or informal, via the phone or Web conferencing or the old-fashioned way: in person. A significant part of managing your job and workload is putting a strategy in place for deciding which meetings to attend and doing everything in your power to make the ones you go to as efficient and productive as possible.

How do you decide if you really need to be at the meeting at all, and if you don't, how do you get out of it? I've worked hard with many business folks on creating criteria for making to-go-or-not-to-go meeting decisions, and it really boils down to asking yourself these four questions: What's the real purpose of the meeting? Who is calling the meeting? If you want to skip the meeting, how well can you make the case for getting out of it? Do you need to send someone in your place if you aren't going to attend?

Of course, your answers will largely depend on your particular circumstances. It will be different for each and every person or case. But let's take a very basic example. If the CEO of your company is calling a meeting with five division heads, of which you are one—be it to talk about the business or his newfound cause rescuing pink salamanders from the Australian outback—common sense dictates that you bend over backward to be there. If you aren't going to show up, make it very clear that you at least tried and consider sending an envoy in your place. On the other end of the spectrum, if you are a sales account executive and the head of sales calls a meeting, you might have a little more latitude. If the purpose is to discuss a radical change in strategy for the company, you best make every attempt to be there. If it's a meeting to discuss the second half of the year, you might, depending on your workload, be able to wiggle your way out of it if you can convince your boss that it's more important for you to get sales for the first half of the year in the bag. What often works best when trying to wiggle out of a meeting is to put a price tag on your attendance by presenting a quick cost-benefit analysis to your boss. In the case of Clarence, the account executive, the argument went something like this: "I have three million dollars in outstanding orders that I need to wrap up today, otherwise we might miss out on those revenues hitting the books this quarter." It was a no-brainer for his boss, who went to the meeting instead of Clarence and reported back to him!

COMMON SENSE IS FAR TOO UNCOMMON.

As I write these final words of advice on getting the job done, it's hard to decide which of many tales to share next. Just as I think one takes the cake in underscoring the lack of common sense in the workplace, I'm reminded of another.

While I'm deciding, let's start with the definition of common sense: a reasonable common understanding between people that translates into sensible action based on the presumed facts of a situation. Now let's play pretend for a second, using a very basic example. You are my assistant and I hand you a letter while saying that it's very urgent and needs to be mailed out immediately. I presume that our reasonable common understanding is that you are going to:

- Put it in an envelope.

- Write the correct address on it.

- Send it out today via the fastest service available.

Okay, what's the big deal, you ask? Well, in Stella's case, in exactly this same situation, her college-educated assistant sent the letter out by regular mail. Yes, as in snail mail, the route our annual holiday card takes to Uncle Bill in North Dakota. Why didn't she send it overnight or at least priority mail? Because, as the assistant explained, Stella didn't specify that she send it out that way. Excuse me, you might ask, are you kidding? As Stella noted, "The truth is, lots of people out there are book smart but life dumb. They cannot think themselves out of a paper bag without instructions." This kind of stuff happens day in and day out at companies across the nation and on a much grander scale than Stella's letter, costing companies millions of dollars in lost revenue or opportunities and causing professionals unimaginable hours of stress and frustration.

So how do you gain a more commonsense approach to your work? One way is to take a larger, forest-through-the-trees view by recognizing the real value and importance of what you do. To keep it simple, let's go back to Stella's assistant. If there was any doubt in her mind about what Stella meant by saying the letter was urgent, the assistant should have asked, "It sounds like this letter needs to get there right away. I am going to send it overnight. Is that okay?" Likewise, given the importance of getting the letter to the person immediately, Stella herself could have been more explicit when giving directions by saying that she wanted it to go out using expedited delivery.

On the face of it, the assistant's job is to attend to the administrative details, in this particular instance to mail an urgent letter.

But if the assistant had considered the larger picture, she would have understood that her work helps Stella, the head of a major division, manage and grow a critical part of the company. The real value of the assistant's work is making sure that things go as smoothly as possible for Stella so that the department can be successful. If the assistant had applied this kind of commonsense thinking to her job, then I bet she would have made a different decision about the letter. Often, common sense is simply saying what you think everyone already knows, just to make sure that everyone really does.

When it comes to common senselessness, though, here's the story that takes the cake.

A twenty-eight-year-old HR wunderkind from a major Fortune 500 company came highly recommended and was recruited by the CEO of a small, yet rapidly expanding firm. Two months into his new post, Mr. Wunderkind started sending a continual stream of amorous e-mails and voice mails to an employee in the company. Needless to say, the employee couldn't believe this was happening, especially coming from the HR director, the very person who is entrusted with protecting the workers from exactly this sort of thing. She asked him to stop, and when he didn't, she rightfully filed harassment charges.

When approached about the situation by the higher-ups, Mr. Wunderkind acted surprised, then denied everything. One week later, a hearing was held with the COO, the accused, another HR professional, and the employee who was making the charges. Saved e-mails and voice mails were produced that undeniably substantiated her harassment claim, forcing his immediate firing and ultimately costing the company thousands of dollars in settlement damages. At the end of the hearing, the COO got up and said to Mr. Wunderkind in a loud whisper, "When I hired you as the HR director, I intended for you to be sitting right here next to me representing us, not on the other side of the table defending yourself."

Maybe the short definition for common sense is simply this: not being stupid.

Three

WHEN YOU OPEN YOUR MOUTH . . . AND THEN SOME

- Listening is part art, part science, and all important.

- Adjust your communication accordingly.

- Say the magic words: *please, thank you,* and *I'm sorry.*

- Keep your mouth shut.

- Get smart about asking dumb questions.

- Learn how to present without needing beta-blockers.

Say the word *communication* and the first thing that comes to mind is all of that cool new technology that has revolutionized the business world. While no doubt e-mail, instant messaging, and Web conferencing have made connecting with each other faster and easier, we still have a long way to go when it comes to mastering one of the most important soft skills of all: being an effective communicator. I would venture to say that nine times out of ten, what these new modes have really given us are simply more opportunities to blow it! But there's one thing for certain: whether you are addressing one or one thousand people—face-to-face, on the phone, or through the wires—your communication skills or lack thereof can make or break your career.

Everything—and I do mean everything—communicates. From how well you listen to others to how well you ask questions, from shaking with stage fright to minding your manners—everything you say and do (or don't!) becomes part of the message. With hectic schedules, multitasking lives, and overflowing in-boxes, people today have the attention spans of gnats. Making matters even worse, you're likely to be communicating with someone who just started working for the company or with a person online whom you've never met. The old days of having months or even years to build trusting relationships with clients and colleagues are over. We no longer have the benefit of history and common understanding to draw on during our interactions.

Despite our having gone high-tech in our communication methods, the basics still matter more than ever—and you'll find out why in this chapter. Through a number of lessons from the trenches, I'll highlight the key soft skills from under the communication umbrella: keeping your ears open, knowing the communication preferences of others and adjusting your message so it has the greatest impact, minding your manners on a number of fronts, asking the right questions, and getting over the jitters so you can present with confidence.

LISTENING IS PART ART, PART SCIENCE, AND ALL IMPORTANT.

I recently read a statistic that during primary-care office visits, patients are interrupted by their doctor an average of eighteen seconds after being asked how they are. A shockingly short amount of time, no? And, of course, this problem doesn't just happen in examining rooms. We've all heard spouses shouting at each other or kids yelling to their parents, "You never listen to me!"

Contrary to how people generally behave, listening is an activity—not just something to do while waiting your turn to speak. Most of us jump in with our own opinions, thoughts, and ideas before the person we are listening to can even finish a sentence. Worse yet are what I call the extra-octane PowerPoint presentations that are overpowering with way too many slides and leave little or no time for listening to what the client might be feeling or needing.

As Jon, a thirty-eight-year-old sales executive, revealed, "Peggy, one lesson I wish I had learned earlier was to stop talking and start listening. But ironically, I never listened to that advice!" Jon explained he was so oriented toward telling others what his firm could offer that he often missed hearing from the client what he really needed to know.

Jon finally learned his lesson the hard way during a presentation that has stuck in his mind ever since. Along with two other more senior people from his firm, he was presenting to an affluent husband-and-wife team. The goal was to land the management of their sizable portfolio. Jon introduced himself and presented the agenda for the day. Halfway into launching into his monologue, he noticed the pair shifting in their chairs and exchanging glances.

Jon looked over at the other two members of his team for direction. "What was even more pathetic is that neither one of them even noticed what was happening. They had their eyes glued to the deck of materials we brought that outlined our firm's services."

Finally, Jon asked the couple if they had any questions. "Yes," the husband replied, "Don't you want to know what type of portfolio we already have and if it's working for us?" Jon responded along the lines of "Oh, I thought you were here for x, y, and z." The wife shot back, "That's not what we had in mind at all. Where did you get that information?"

Needless to say, there were some red faces in the room when all was said and done. Incorrect assumptions had been made all the way around, because no one had bothered to tune in to the communication station WIFT-FM (What's In It For Them?).

Much of business happens during various kinds of social interaction. And to be successful, these interactions not only depend on listening to the message, but equally on creating a shared meaning with the other person. This process takes time, patience, and curiosity—all of which are in short supply in today's fast-paced world. So to ensure that you really understand what the other person is saying, here are some things you can do:

- Remain silent until the other person has finished. After she stops, ask for clarification with a question like "Let me be sure that I understand what you're saying." Then paraphrase her words to see if you've gotten it right.

- Be curious instead of defensive. Eagerly and excitedly, ask the other person to add more specifics so you can truly understand what she means.

- Use both nonverbal and verbal cues to convey understanding and empathy, such as nodding your head in agreement and saying things like "I understand how you could feel that way," or "Please, tell me more."

The way we listen and respond strongly influences how others respond to us. We all want to feel that we are being listened to. When people believe we are trying to understand their feelings and intentions, they become more comfortable sharing their ideas and thoughts with us. You will do just fine if you follow the Do's and Don'ts of Listening:

DO . . .

- Keep an open mind.

- Listen attentively for the total meaning.

- Tune into the feelings of the speaker along with the facts.

- Be present and focused.

- Stay attentive to nonverbal cues.

- Ask the right questions at the right time.

- Pay attention to both content and delivery.

- Know what your hot buttons are and don't let them rule your behavior.

- Listen with your heart along with your head.

DON'T . . .

- Make assumptions or prejudgments.

- Try to fill "airtime."

- Interrupt with your thoughts or advice.

- Interrogate.

- Preach.

- Take the subject off into another direction.

- Multitask or let your mind wander.

ADJUST YOUR COMMUNICATION ACCORDINGLY.

Syreeta was frustrated. She was under deadline and needed her new boss to make some key decisions about a major project. But each time she tried to share her detailed analysis, which she planned to follow with recommendations, he looked away and started fidgeting before she could get past the opening comments. His attention had already wandered to something else and Syreeta could tell the encounter was going nowhere fast.

"Reverse the order and put the punch line first," I advised.

"What?" she said with an incredulous look, adding, "I worked on that analysis day and night. I want him to see what a good job I did looking at the various markets. He just needs to pay attention to what I'm telling him."

"Syreeta, more important, you need to pay attention to how he can best hear you. Right now you are coming across like static on his television screen. Make it easier for him to tune in and cut your entire presentation in half."

When it comes to communicating, whether with one person or a hundred, act like a chameleon and gear your message to the needs of your audience. It's an incredibly simple concept, but one that can change your life.

In Syreeta's case, her boss was an extremely busy guy—he had even been sending e-mails to her in the middle of the night. As head of distribution for a huge manufacturing conglomerate, he was handling the responsibilities of several jobs and felt inundated. No wonder it was so hard to hold his attention. Furthermore, he was Syreeta's third boss in as many years. She barely knew the guy. Had they been working together longer, she probably would have already figured out what it took to get through to him.

Syreeta clearly needed a new strategy and approach. Beating her head against the wall was getting her nothing more than a sore head and the boss's ire. So the next time, she trimmed her presentation down to the bones and started off by quickly stating her recommendations, which she followed with a brief summary of her most critical findings. Once Syreeta's boss had a good sense of the headline and the bottom line, he was able to focus on the details of the plan and give her the input she needed.

Before you tell someone something, scope out his communication-style preferences. Does he like slow and methodical or quick and summarized? Does he want to ride above the details or dive into them? Does he prefer daily e-mails, as-needed voice mails, or once-a-week phone or face-to-face updates? Asking all these questions from the get-go could have saved Syreeta a lot of time and grief.

SAY THE MAGIC WORDS: *PLEASE, THANK YOU,* AND *I'M SORRY.*

Which sentence do you think sounds better and will most likely result in a more timely response?

Send me the report.

Or:

Please send me the report. Thanks!

Whatever mode you're using to communicate in business or in life, the magic words are the same: *please, thank you,* and *I'm sorry.* Just like your grandma probably told you, using please and thank you are great habits to get into. Trust me when I say that employing them daily in your verbal and written communication will take you far. They are also easy to incorporate, so just do it.

"I'm sorry," on the other hand, is a little bit trickier. People often have a hard time mastering the art of the apology or of simply taking responsibility for their mistakes. Few of us want to admit we've done something that lets others down. In many cultures, it's all important to save face, making apologizing all the more difficult. But even when that's not the case, who wants to be wrong?

Yet failing to apologize occurs all too often. Like when someone accidentally sent an e-mail to someone who shouldn't have seen it. That's exactly what happened with Jason's e-mail to his girlfriend, Kelly, whose singing career he recently started managing. Unfortunately, he pressed "Reply to All" and it mistakenly went out to Kelly's publicist, Tamika, as well.

The e-mail said something like this:

"Don't tell Tamika, but if she doesn't get major media within the next month, we will stop paying."

Tamika was shocked. She had a long-standing working relationship of mutual respect and trust with Kelly going all the way back to her second album. Since the success of that effort, Tamika had promoted several other albums and concerts for Kelly over the years.

So what did Kelly do when Tamika brought Jason's e-mail to her attention? Not much. "She brushed me off and acted like I was making a big deal out of nothing for even bringing it up."

Did Jason at least extend an olive branch?

No, although throughout the rest of the project, he continued to send e-mails to Tamika as if nothing had ever happened.

And what happened to the working relationship between Kelly and Tamika?

"It was never the same again after that," said Tamika. "The incident cast Kelly in an entirely different light. Like the air in a pinpricked balloon, the trust drained out of our relationship. In retrospect, all it would have taken to prevent this was a simple apology."

While this story might seem like a cautionary tale of being careful before you hit Send and about never saying anything in an e-mail that you wouldn't mind the whole world reading, it's really about one of the most old-fashioned things in the world: knowing when to apologize.

And don't give me the excuse, "But Peggy, this person works for me and I pay her, so why do I have to say that I am sorry?" Well, guess what? In the end, we are all just people. Asking forgiveness may not smooth over every mistake, but it's always a good place to start.

Yes, it really can be that simple.

KEEP YOUR MOUTH SHUT.

Just as common courtesy is a big plus and will never go out of style, the same can be said of good table manners. "What?" you might say. "I thought keeping your mouth shut was going to be about listening more." Well, it means that, too, which I already covered early on this chapter. But since I've just discussed the importance of nonverbal communication, here's a big one from the same category that deserves special attention all of its own. It was inspired in part by a horse's mouth.

A longtime client of mine worked in private banking for a very prestigious firm. As a favor to a CEO from one of her major corporate accounts, she agreed to meet and have lunch with his just-about-to-graduate-from-a-very-expensive-college daughter to help open doors for her at firms on Wall Street.

"She chewed her food just like a horse, Peggy. You know, when it's munching an apple and all you can see are those giant gums and teeth. That's how she chewed every bite. Worse yet, she was also a smacker!" My client continued to explain, "Even if you turned away to avoid looking into her mouth, you couldn't help hearing her eat!" Given that my client could never recommend anyone with those kinds of table manners, especially in a line of work that entailed dealing with such high-end clients and often dining at the finest establishments, we spent the next half hour determining how best to communicate the truth to the CEO father without offending him.

Bad table manners are no longer a rare occurrence by any means, which explains the flurry of workshops being offered to corporate types these days on all aspects of etiquette. People bring to meals—and, of course, other situations as well—a variety of deplorable manners. Unfortunately, the issue seems to cross the lines of position, income, and age. I'll leave you with a story that takes the cake—even topping the horse—when it comes to keeping your mouth shut. This tale is about a family who performed a "clean up your table manners" intervention on a loved one.

"It was my sixty-six-year-old father," said forty-three-year-old Hilary, explaining, "My parents have a lot of annoying habits, so I just put up with my dad's less-than-ideal table manners." Hilary had never thought about this limiting him business-wise until her seventeen-year-old daughter mentioned the subject following the family's Thanksgiving dinner. As Hilary recalled, "On our long drive home, my daughter said, 'Mom, it's disgusting how Grandpa opens his mouth when he chews. He's this big executive, hobnobbing all over the place and attending countless dinners and banquets. He could be dining with the president of the United States and chewing with his mouth open. How embarrassing.'" Her daughter's comment hit Hilary like a ton of bricks. Although her father was always impeccably groomed and dressed, his less-than-stellar table manners could be hurting his image and someone should just tell him, once and for all. So a month later, after relentless prodding from Hilary's daughter, the two performed an intervention on their next visit. "I'm ashamed to say that I let my daughter do most of the talking," Hilary said. "Telling someone he has bad manners at his age was the equivalent of pointing out a piece of spinach stuck in your front teeth for fifty years!"

And what was his reaction?

He was incredulous at first and more than a little bit defensive. But once he chewed on the truth (pun intended) of what his granddaughter was saying, he was mortified. Fortunately, he was able to make the fix immediately. "That was three years ago, and he has been tight-lipped, so to speak, ever since," Hilary reported, adding, "When he finally digested my daughter's feedback, I knew exactly what he was silently wishing: Why didn't someone tell me . . . *sooner?*"

GET SMART ABOUT ASKING DUMB QUESTIONS.

The old cliché that "there are no dumb questions" is true in that we can always learn from others. That's why when we hold back from asking questions out of a fear of being perceived as stupid by our supervisors or peers, we greatly limit our opportunity to grow. Even worse, we risk embarrassing ourselves when we move ahead without being adequately informed. After all, the only thing worse than sounding stupid is actually acting stupidly by not knowing enough about what you are doing or saying.

At the same time, as countless executives have pointed out to me over the years, you *do* have to be careful about how you ask, who you ask, and when you ask. On top of that, make sure that before you ask at all, someone hasn't already told you the answer—in which case it's no longer about coming across as dumb, but about coming across as unprepared. For example, many of my clients complain about being in meetings in which someone asks a question that is clearly answered in the first paragraph of the briefing document distributed in advance of the meeting. They also disdain people who miss out, for whatever reason, on previous discussions and don't bother to catch up later in private—especially when they waste valuable group time rehashing things. As one senior manager recently told me, "People need to bring themselves up to speed and come prepared for *all* their meetings, not just the ones with the big bosses."

While being careful about how you go about asking is important, don't become so vigilant that you end up tongue-tied and refrain from speaking up at all. One senior executive confided in me that he was scared to death to ask questions at meetings with the CEO, whom he reported to directly. He didn't want to come across as a slow thinker by bringing up things that the boss might have already thought through. What the executive didn't realize was that the CEO—who did indeed process things quite rapidly—relied on him for a more careful and in-depth analysis of situations. This so-called slow thinking was exactly the kind of questioning that the boss wanted to hear.

Forty-seven-year-old Tammy, a successful freelance business writer, told me a revealing coming-of-age story from her fast-track years working in brand marketing for a major Fortune 500 company. As a newly minted MBA, Tammy had been recruited to work as an assistant to the brand manager on a major packaged goods product. Her boss, years her senior and a real taskmaster, asked her to provide some simple financial projections for him to present to the account's director at an upcoming meeting. The boss assumed—given her MBA from a prestigious school—that Tammy's forecasts would be spot on. Unfortunately for everyone, they were anything but. In front of the director and the entire brand team, Tammy's boss had to backpedal on the spot to explain several discrepancies in the figures she had provided to him. Tammy was mortified and felt her face go white as she listened to him correct her work in front of everyone. While preparing the projections, she had wondered if some of her assumptions might have been incorrect. But Tammy had been too afraid to ask her boss for help for fear of appearing stupid. "Peggy, I wish someone had told me that if I was feeling too insecure to ask my boss, at least I should have asked someone else, like a colleague at work or a buddy from grad school whom I could trust with my seemingly dumb questions."

LEARN HOW TO PRESENT WITHOUT NEEDING BETA-BLOCKERS.

Public speaking is the number one fear in America. Death is number two. Therefore, according to comedian Jerry Seinfeld, at a funeral most Americans would rather be the one in the casket than the one giving the eulogy. Funny, but all too true. Be it a top corporate executive speaking to employees, a best man toasting the bride and groom, or a mom battling an issue at a school board meeting, public speaking strikes fear in most of us.

My client Angela is a case in point. Despite her incredible career trajectory, she has suffered silently behind the scenes with presentation anxiety since childhood. In her first job, she was asked to give a talk at a conference, which had her worrying for weeks. As the date closed in, Angela began waking up several times during the night; and on the morning of the presentation, she was so sick to her stomach that she ended up being a no-show.

Not wanting to repeat that ghastly situation ever again, Angela developed endless ways to worm out of giving talks. She managed to dodge the bullet for years. By midcareer, Angela was delegating big internal presentations and industry conference panels to colleagues or direct reports. She was able to get away with avoiding giving big presentations until her company was bought, leaving her among the last ones standing from the former firm and in a very visible position. It soon became clear that she was going to be responsible for flying to Switzerland on a regular basis to update the board on the integration process. Panic ensued.

The first time Angela flew to Basel, she resorted to borrowing her husband's blood pressure medicine (a beta-blocker, which some people take for performance anxiety) and using it before the meeting. Although she was lucky not to have an adverse reaction to the medication and was able to give her report without passing out, Angela was already dreading the next trip. That's when she finally admitted to herself that her speaking phobia was completely out of hand and gave me an SOS call.

While Angela's situation represents an extreme, some people claim to be at the other end of the spectrum, saying they never get nervous when presenting. I've learned not to believe them. They're either in denial or taking drugs—something akin to beta-blockers—to calm themselves down. That's because *everyone* gets butterflies or an adrenaline rush in one type of speaking situation or another. What triggers the anxiety is different for each of us. Some people don't like to go in front of a few colleagues, but have no problem with strangers. Others are fine presenting in front of really big audiences and less comfortable talking to smaller crowds. One client was okay when presenting to a room of ten or fewer, but adding an eleventh person did him in. A CEO I coached had no problem speaking before five thousand in a Greek arena, but melted down when in front of thirty senior managers.

Regardless of the trigger, start overcoming anxiousness by identifying your "butterfly spots." Figure out which situations or people make you nervous, then develop a strategy for warding the nerves off ahead of time. However, unlike some coaches, one strategy I *don't* advise is to imagine your audience naked. I tried that once and ended up in an uncontrollable fit of giggles. Often by simply becoming self-aware and seeing how irrational your fears are, you will weaken their power over you. The best nerve-management tool I've ever found is to be prepared. Whatever you do, don't delay thinking about everything until the night before an important communication event. If you avoid planning ahead, I guarantee you'll be operating from the most inefficient mode of all: panic. Be sure to give yourself plenty of time to consider the audience, prepare your content, and become comfortable delivering the material.

First, start by tuning in to your listeners' favorite communication station. As I mentioned previously, it's called WIFT-FM (for What's In It For Them?). Identify the potential needs, objectives, and goals of your audience. Why are they there and listening to you in the first place?

After you sort that out, take the emotional temperature of the audience by asking yourself, "What thoughts and feelings might they be bringing with them? Will they be happy to be there? Ready to have a good time? Tired? Bored? Frustrated? Overworked? Angry at a new initiative or change that's taking place at the company? Scared about losing their jobs?"

Next, determine the point of your message. What do you want the audience to think, feel, and do after you've spoken with them? Your own goals must be specific and actionable. Avoid namby-pamby generalities like "I want the clients to have a better understanding of what we do." Instead, think along the lines of "At the end of this meeting, I want them to lean across the table and say, 'We want to do business with you.'"

After asking yourself these questions, make sure that the content you prepare will both meet your goals and be interesting to the listener. Shape the message into stories that are filled with vivid images, specific examples, appropriate humor, and passion. Avoid reciting laundry lists of facts. Keep things brief, but not so brief that you leave out crucial information.

And last, but definitely not least, rehearse, rehearse, rehearse. Retreat to a quiet place where you can walk around to loosen up and generate some energy. Do not—repeat, do not—practice in front of a mirror because that will tend to make you self-conscious and stiff. As you walk, read the words of your presentation out loud a few times, just to get them what I call "out on your tongue." The first time you say written words, they rarely come out the way you expect or want them to sound. So say them aloud and then practice paraphrasing the information in various ways until the words roll out naturally and conversationally, as if you were talking to a good friend over a cup of coffee. Once you are able to come across as spontaneous, you will sound more entertaining and become someone people really want to listen to.

A classic study by Dr. Albert Mehrabian of UCLA showed that 55 percent of the message received by an audience is conveyed by one's physical appearance, which includes—in addition to the obvious things like clothes, hairstyle, and makeup—your gestures, facial animation, smile, posture, and eye contact. Your vocal characteristics and variation—tone, pitch, pause, speed, and volume—constitute 38 percent of what the audience takes in. This leaves a mere 7 percent for content, or what I call "the facts, ma'am." On the 1950s television show *Dragnet,* the investigator always bottom-lined his inquiry to witnesses by insisting they give him "just the facts, ma'am, just the facts." But Dr. Mehrabian's study contradicts the *Dragnet* approach and makes it clear that a dull presentation is unlikely to persuade or convince anyone. Now, don't get me wrong, you *do* need to be knowledgeable about your subject and get the facts straight, but no one will be paying much attention to those facts—let alone be won over to your point of view—without a dynamic and engaging delivery.

And what, you may be wondering, ever happened to my client's presentation anxiety? Well, since we started working together, she has given reports at six more board meetings. Angela says that although she probably will never love speaking to groups, at least now she can do it without getting sick or resorting to serious avoidance behavior. And in her charmingly modest way she adds, "Well, they haven't thrown tomatoes at me yet, so I guess I'm doing just fine!"

Four

HANDLING YOUR CRITICS

- Books are judged by their covers and the same is true for you.

- Don't be the last one to find out how you're doing.

- Never tolerate a bully boss—even if you have to quit.

- You don't need to be everyone's best friend—that's what dogs are for.

- Your greatest tormentor might prove to be your greatest teacher.

- Know where to draw the line between self-improvement and self-destruction.

- Stay cool in the hot seat.

I am always surprised by the reaction of my clients when I tell them they are being judged all the time at work. At first they give me that "Of course, Peggy" look, but then the reality of what I'm saying begins to seep in. I can see the terror on their faces. Did she really mean *all the time,* as in not just during performance reviews and presentations? Did she mean from the moment I walk through the office door? Would that even include those Mondays when, half awake, I stumbled through the early morning conference with my boss?

Yes. Yes. Yes. And yes.

We are sizing up people and situations every minute of every day in our business lives. Sometimes our impressions are good, sometimes bad, but rarely if ever neutral. Whether we want to admit it or not, we are just as often on the receiving end of being sized up by everyone around us, including colleagues, bosses, and clients. Most people don't like to think about this for the simple reason that being judged often goes hand in hand with being criticized. And who likes to hear about their shortfalls, real or perceived?

When it comes to being judged, though, the last thing you want to do is to stick your head in the sand. As it is sometimes said, you can avoid criticism by doing nothing, saying nothing, and being nothing. Of course, then you'll be criticized for being a do-nothing blob. So avoiding action is not the answer. As anybody who has ever been a success at anything will attest, we often learn more from our mistakes than our successes.

The lessons in this chapter will focus on a variety of soft skills associated with critics and criticism, including the importance of first and lasting impressions in person, over the phone, and in writing; keeping your antenna raised; developing conflict-resolution techniques for dealing with difficult people—whether a bully boss or contentious colleague; striking the right balance when it comes to your desire to be liked; preparing for and keeping your cool during performance reviews; and managing the hands-down worst critic of all: *you*!

BOOKS ARE JUDGED BY THEIR COVERS AND THE SAME IS TRUE FOR YOU.

Growing up, I'm sure you heard on more than one occasion "Never judge a book by its cover." Or, in other words, don't judge someone or something only by its appearance.

While no doubt a noble goal, by now you've probably observed that it's one that's rarely met, especially in business, where people are always sizing up each other and first impressions are everything—and I do mean everything.

Within the first one-thousandth of a second of meeting you, those on the receiving end have already started clicking off judgments about you. Within seven seconds, they're trying to determine whether they like you, if they trust you, or if you appear confident and qualified. If they can't decide within that time frame, they spend the next thirty to sixty seconds going through a critical laundry list in their heads about you: Do you have a command of your subject? Are you ready for that upcoming promotion? Are you even competent? And remember, it's never too late to make a bad impression, even on someone who already knows and likes you. If you enter a meeting with a scowl on your face, your colleagues might wonder if you've just heard some bad, work-related news. With each interaction, they will continue their assessment of you. So that's why one of the best ways to handle criticism is to avoid it in the first place by paying careful attention to how you are coming across to others.

Even when you aren't meeting others face-to-face, first impressions still count. In today's virtual world, you will be judged for speaking too loudly and quickly—or softly and slowly—on the telephone or by your spelling errors and incorrect word usage when writing. As Dale, an executive coaching client of mine, recently said, "There's nothing worse than reading e-mails full of careless spelling and grammatical mistakes from supposedly well-educated colleagues." He went on to mention some of the ones that bug him the most:

- there/their/they're

- its/it's

- your/you're

- whether/weather

- to/too/two

- waste/waist

- accept/except

When people write to Dale inquiring about a job opportunity and he see these types of mistakes, their résumés head directly to the trash can.

Thanks to better and more cost-efficient technology, people are using videoconferencing for everything from job interviews to global brainstorming sessions. Sometimes in these types of meetings, people forget they are on camera and get caught in unflattering acts, from picking at their teeth to nodding off. You never know when the camera will be on you, so be on your best behavior from the moment you put your toe in the room.

Whether in a videoconference or up close and in person, you are always on stage and making an impression of one sort or another—a point that seemed lost on a woman I recently ran into at the airport. Hours earlier, she had been an attendee at the workshop I had given at a women's leadership conference. Seated with a group of her coworkers at the bar, she waved me over to say how much she liked my session. It was the first time we had talked one-on-one, although she had spoken up several times during the workshop. I thanked her for her comments. Then one of her friends piped up, saying, "Niki is the 'big mouth' in our company meetings, always asking things the rest of us want to know but are afraid to ask." Niki concurred and told me that, in fact, she had just gotten a tattoo of the words "big mouth." Before I knew what she was doing, she flipped up the back of her jacket, pulled down the waistband of her pants, and showed me the new tattoo on the upper-right-hand side of her butt. All I could say was "Wow" before quickly excusing myself to find another place to wait for my flight.

Inappropriate behavior can run the gamut from public displays of tattoos that are located in places the sun doesn't shine (which I didn't even have on my list until Niki) to getting sloshed at a business affair. A senior editor at a major publishing house let down her guard upon having a few drinks too many at an after-work networking event. One of her younger colleagues from the same company was appalled as Ms. Tipsy went on and on like some shock jock. She shouted over the hum of the event, telling everyone at their table about what was *really* going on behind the scenes at the company. Her colleague, who until that moment had a generally good impression of her, never looked at her quite the same way again. While people might excuse that one holiday party occurrence, drinking too much with clients and colleagues—especially when coupled with a bad case of loose lips— has left many people with perpetual career hangovers. Don't be the next victim. It's never too late to make a bad impression, even on someone who already knows and likes you.

DON'T BE THE LAST ONE TO FIND OUT HOW YOU'RE DOING.

A stalling or derailing career is often the result of not knowing how others *really* view your personality and performance. Maybe you thought someone would just come out and tell you. Maybe your philosophy is that no news is good news. Or perhaps you have such a high opinion of yourself that you can't imagine anyone would think you weren't terrific. That was exactly Stuart's problem. All his life, this Gen X graduate of the best schools had been told by his parents how fabulous he was, which led him to believe his own hype. Until, that is, an HR person informed him right before an upcoming performance review that the head of his group wasn't so impressed. How could that be, Stuart wondered? Hadn't he brought in a ton of business for the firm? It turned out that while his boss hadn't wanted to disrupt the golden goose, she was sitting on some serious complaints about how Stuart had handled a particular situation. Had Stuart's feedback antenna been up, or had he thought to ask how he was doing, he wouldn't have been the last to know and could have nipped things in the bud. But now his boss was unhappy and Stuart's bonus was on the line.

The whole process of giving and receiving feedback is understandably scary. On the giving side, we all want to be liked, and so most of us will sidestep confrontational situations whenever possible. After all, what could be more conflict producing than giving a negative evaluation of someone else's performance? On the receiving end, who really enjoys sitting in the hot seat while being told how they've screwed up? If like most of us you tend toward the no-news-is-good-news direction, then it's time to reset your default mode. You really *do* want to know on a regular basis how you are being perceived by others, especially when the news isn't good. By encouraging and welcoming feedback, you can make adjustments accordingly as you go rather than being taken by surprise at your next performance review. You don't want to miss out on this direct path to personal and professional improvement. Furthermore, fessing up and admitting your mistakes lessens the opportunity for others to be critical of you at unsuspecting moments.

A great example of this is something we've all experienced: waiting in a checkout line for way too long. When it's finally your turn, you are so steamed up that you are about to launch into a very unfriendly diatribe. But the clerk turns to you and says with great sincerity, "I'm so sorry about your wait. We are down to two salespeople today and I really appreciate your patience. What can I do for you?" You want to say sarcastically with a snarl, "How about giving me this cashmere sweater for free?" Her apology is so genuine, though, that you don't. It's hard to bite her head off after she acknowledged your long wait and took responsibility for the inconvenience. So you respond instead with "Oh, that's okay, don't worry about it."

When it comes to soliciting feedback, where do you begin? First, let your boss, your direct reports, and your colleagues all know that you welcome their input whether positive or critical. Making it clear that you are open and receptive will encourage them to tell you what they think before things get out of hand. Of course, when they take you up on your offer, you better be ready to hear their input without becoming defensive. Carefully listen to everything they say, ask questions, and invite them to make specific suggestions of ways you could improve your behavior. When responding to their feedback, be sure to communicate your opinions using nonemotional and nonjudgmental language.

One client, a CFO, recently ran into one of her former bosses at Chicago's O'Hare airport. Nearly two decades ago, he had been her manager at the firm where she started out as a junior accountant. Since both of their flights were delayed, they headed to the nearest lounge for a drink and to catch up. While filling her in on developments in his life and at the company during the last twenty years, he casually mentioned that she had been hands down one of the best young people he had ever supervised. "Peggy, why didn't he tell that to me back then? I can't remember him ever saying anything positive to me during the three years we worked together." I pointed out that she could have initiated the feedback herself at any time by simply asking him how she was doing and if he was satisfied with her progress. "It never occurred to me to do that," she said. "At the beginning of my career, I lived in a stress-induced frenzy, fearing that I wasn't good enough. I lacked self-confidence and didn't want to open myself up for target practice. Besides, he was the boss. Wasn't it up to him to tell me if I was doing a good job? Believe me, knowing how he felt back then would have saved me a lot of sleepless nights and premature gray hairs!"

NEVER TOLERATE A BULLY BOSS— EVEN IF YOU HAVE TO QUIT.

Do encounters with your boss have a lot in common with falling into a cactus patch? That's exactly how I felt when approaching division head Madeline, an extremely prickly person on the outside who in true bully-boss fashion proved to be anything but on the inside. I'm not going to lie—she was one of the few people I've ever coached whom I didn't like when I first met her. From the get-go, she came across as nasty and offensive. While greeting her at our initial session, I mistakenly called her Melanie, the name of another client at the firm with whom I had worked earlier that same day. If looks and vocal tone could kill, I would have instantly met my demise then and there from the wrath of Madeline—just for mixing up my *M* names.

By all accounts, Madeline was very, very smart. So smart, in fact, that she was able to explain away virtually anything that had gone wrong for her on the job since joining the company two years ago. Madeline blamed everything and everyone from a malfunctioning and poorly designed computer system to a bunch of lazy, brainless underlings—not to mention an inept boss to boot.

But here's one thing that Madeline, with all her smarts, didn't grasp: she was on the verge of getting canned. A mere nanosecond away from being pushed out the door, she was being given one more chance by her boss. He and the HR director had called me in as a last-ditch effort to do the dirty work that they should have taken care of themselves a long time ago: to address the growing list of complaints about Madeline's behavior—everything from yelling at her assistant for making a mistake to berating colleagues in front of clients.

After listening to her spew venom for most of an hour, I interrupted her diatribe. "Madeline, I need to stop you here so I can tell you what I am thinking right now, which I imagine is similar to what your boss and colleagues feel, which is, quite frankly, why we are here today. First, you greeted me with a very snappish and nasty hello after I mistakenly called you Melanie. Then you continued with the unpleasantness even after I was extremely contrite and apologized three times, explaining how I had just finished working with a client named Melanie who was evidently still on my mind when I opened the door to greet you. Since then, you've spent the last hour denigrating absolutely everyone in your office without taking one ounce of responsibility for anything that's happened or being at all curious as to why people react to you the way they do. I'm telling you in no uncertain terms that if you don't start examining your behavior and changing how you interact, not only will I refuse to work with you, but so will everyone else!"

For the first thirty seconds after I finished talking, Madeline said nothing at all. The room was so quiet that I worried she had stopped breathing. Suddenly, the expression on her face went from prickly cactus to soft marshmallow. Bursting into tears, Madeline told me that she didn't want to be so mean. Between sobs, she explained that her husband—whom she called the nicest guy on earth—always saw the glass half full, while she thought it was half empty. But although Madeline knew she could be difficult—her siblings certainly had no problem letting her know this fact—she was completely unaware that the people at work were so unhappy with her. "Maybe I was the last to know because my colleagues were afraid to approach me," she speculated.

There are many types of difficult managers, but the most common is the bully boss. The bully boss's modus operandi often involves the following kind of thinking: "They'll never get rid of me because I bring in so much money for the firm," or "I can do whatever I want because I'm the best they've got." And in the past, that kind of thinking was likely to work. Companies often overlooked this kind of behavior because the bullies made significant contributions as employees. In recent years, however, fewer companies are willing to put up with this kind of behavior. They can't afford the high turnover and potential lawsuits. As well, employees today are generally far less likely to tolerate being mistreated by the boss. In many larger firms, bullies are being weeded out at the middle-manager level before they get to the top. Yet worker beware, because they still slip through.

So what do you do if you have a Madeline and your company doesn't take care of the dirty work? Try these strategies for carefully handling the cactus.

Ask yourself, are you truly dealing with a bully? Don't confuse a demanding boss with a bully. Someone who holds you accountable or expects that you arrive on time for work is not a bully. A workplace bully is someone who repeatedly verbally abuses you by screaming at you, belittling you, or humiliating you in front of others. They rarely say they are sorry unless called on the carpet. Even then, their words of apology come with great reluctance, if at all.

Join forces. If you plan to speak up, be willing to get fired or take the repercussions of being frozen out or skipped over for promotions. Before confronting your boss, consider recruiting allies in your effort. Compare notes with coworkers whom you trust. Seek out the support of an HR person, especially if your boss is high up in the company. Consider why your boss is getting away with being a bully in the first place. Is this kind of behavior pervasive in your company, or is it simply a case of one rotten apple? If your situation is the former, this is probably not the place for you to work. If it's the latter, then proceed to the next step.

Nip it in the bud immediately. As your teacher may have told you when you were having problems on the playground, a bully can't bully if you don't let him. Respond to your boss with simple and factual statements along the lines of "In the past two months you have on more than one occasion screamed at me in front of colleagues, saying that I was incompetent, stupid, and didn't deserve my job. Not only are these assertions not true, but this is not the way I expect to be treated in a professional workplace environment. In the future, if you have a problem with the way that I do things, please tell me in a normal tone of voice, without assassinating my character in the process." This sounds so exceedingly simple, but standing up to him or her will earn you respect and can break the pattern of abuse.

No excuses. Don't give the bully boss the benefit of doubt by making excuses for his or her atrocious behavior. Befriending the bully will only encourage the behavior to continue or even escalate.

Talk in private. Bully bosses have a penchant for humiliating others in public. Resist the urge, however, to take the person on then and there. Rarely do they give an inch when in front of an audience. It's best to confront bullying behavior behind closed doors and/or put it in writing.

Avoid psychobabble and focus on specific behaviors. When confronting a bully, stay away from telling them your theories—Freudian, New Age, or any other—about why they act the way they do. Instead, stick to the specific behaviors you want them to change. For example, don't tell your boss, "You always put down everyone else's ideas because of your inferiority complex." It would be far more useful to say, "In yesterday's meeting, you asked for my thoughts on the economic forecast, then proceeded to dismiss my opinions using swear words and a raised voice. In the future, if you have similar complaints, please address them with me privately, and in a civil manner."

Practice being in a Zen-like state. As I often tell clients, if I'm watching someone explode on me, I think to myself, "Okay, Peggy, before you start to react with your own bad temper, just envision this person as a four-year-old child having a tantrum." Once I do that, my own response de-escalates and the intense urge to scream or smack someone passes. Another helpful technique is what I call "being Buddha." Start by breathing slowly and counting to ten. If you are still agitated, count to ten again. Then use a soothing inner monologue, such as "This, too, will pass." If it doesn't and the bullying behavior persists, save yourself a lot of grief and find yourself another job *fast!*

YOU DON'T NEED TO BE EVERYONE'S BEST FRIEND— THAT'S WHAT DOGS ARE FOR.

Most of us have heard someone describe a colleague by saying, "There's something about him that's just *too* nice! *Too* willing to help. *Too* smiley. *Too* always right there. Just *too too!*"

Being perceived as "too nice" breeds mistrust with others and makes you suspect. It can also interfere with your effectiveness and will lose you respect. Don't take me wrong. Likability matters as much in business as it does in the rest of your life. While it's obvious how negative behavior like bullying will limit you, extremes on the other end of the spectrum are equally dangerous.

Being overly nice can lead to your downfall whenever you are in a position where others look to you for guidance—whether you're a manager, a parent, a teacher, or charged with any other leadership role.

The need to be liked is universal. But be sure to temper it with this truth: wanting to be everyone's best friend doesn't always get the job done. This is what Deven, a sales director, wished he had learned sooner. Years ago, he was leading his team through a complex project that challenged everyone's talents and skills. As he said, "Half way through it, killing myself to please everyone, I realized some things. To be an effective leader, you have to be firm, hold your ground, and insist on accountability. You need to recognize that all of that is going to make some people bristle. But it also makes them grow. And if you help someone or your team do that, you will not only earn their respect, but most likely their admiration forever."

Roberto, a college math professor whom I have known for years, reminded me of this yet again. Recently, at a mutual friend's party, I commented to him, "Your students must love you—you're so nice." He looked at me with surprise, then laughed and said, "Love me? Nice? You must be kidding. By mid-term, especially during second semester calculus, they complain I'm the meanest person in the world. They're convinced that my life is devoted to making them miserable. But by the end of the course, when they've finally mastered the difficult content, they're proud of what they've accomplished, and, suddenly, I'm not such a bad guy after all."

Being perceived as "too nice" isn't just a liability for those who are in charge of others, as with Deven or Roberto. A "building backbone" lesson came in handy for my friend Lila when it came time to charge her client.

• • •

Lila was just starting out in her career as an organizational development consultant when one of her clients refused to pay up. She had a signed contract for a two-month project with the company, but after three weeks of work, they decided to cancel. Although pleased with her progress so far, they had a change of plans and no longer needed her services. The cancellation policy they had agreed to required payment of the full amount under these circumstances. Feeling bad about charging them for unused time and wanting to be nice, Lila called Aaron (the person who had initially hired her) and offered to apply the remaining time to another project within the firm. He seemed uninterested in pursuing the suggestion, so she proceeded to send him an invoice for the balance due, along with a friendly note. Two weeks later, Aaron called Lila at her office and angrily berated her for insisting on being paid. She reminded him of the cancellation policy that he had signed and of her offer to make up for the shortfall elsewhere within the company. A long pause followed, then Aaron had the nerve to say, "Well, Lila, I suggest you consider if you would like to work with us in the future and what kind of effect pursuing this further might have on that." His voice was dripping with threat, implying, of course, "You'll never work here again if you make us pay you." Lila was so stunned, all she could think of to say was "Oh, okay, well let me think about that," before hanging up. For several days, she thought seriously about dropping the entire matter, but something about that didn't feel quite right, which is why she called me for advice. After explaining everything to me, Lila commented, "Maybe I'm making too big of a deal about this. I mean, I don't want to lose the chance to get their business in the future."

I asked Lila to consider several things before making a decision about how to handle the situation. First, what was she *really* afraid of? Did she think she would never work again anywhere, for any company? Or was she mainly concerned that Aaron would think she was too demanding and moneygrubbing—in other words, "not nice"? Would she even want to work in the future with this guy who didn't honor his commitments? And how would she feel about her own worth if she gave in?

Was Lila's attachment to being Ms. Nice Gal so strong that she buckled under? No! After a couple of days of mulling over my questions, she composed a letter to Aaron that outlined her position in a firm but positive way. She felt nervous writing it and even more nervous mailing it, wondering if she wasn't being flexible, understanding, or nice enough. But Lila's doubts were ameliorated when she promptly received a check from the company for the amount she had asked for and was rightfully owed. Last report, she hadn't worked for Aaron again but has had plenty of other clients to keep her busy.

YOUR GREATEST TORMENTOR MIGHT PROVE TO BE YOUR GREATEST TEACHER.

We won't like everyone we work with in our careers. Yet sometimes even those people we don't connect with can turn out to be incredible teachers once we learn to combine self-control with a bit of detective work. This is the lesson forty-seven-year-old Miranda reminded me of recently when telling me the story of her participation on a work team that included an older woman named Lauren.

Last year, Miranda was introduced to Lauren through a common friend and business associate, Aileen. Aileen had gone on and on to Lauren about how Miranda would be the perfect addition to the team and how fantastic it would be if they could all work together. Given her complete trust in Aileen's opinion and that the project was running late, Lauren brought in Miranda sight unseen.

The first time they met was over a business lunch with several other team members present. Before anyone had even ordered, Lauren interrupted a story Miranda was telling and in no uncertain terms told her she didn't know what she was talking about.

Although not someone who lets people push her around, Miranda immediately stopped talking and quietly listened through the salad course. By the time the entrées were served, however, she had gently eased her way back into the conversation. "I acted as if nothing had happened, leaving everyone at the table questioning Lauren's behavior instead of mine. I quickly saw that taking her on would make my indignant response the defining act instead of her rudeness. Had this incident happened twenty years ago when I was just starting out, I would have taken the incident personally and confronted her on the spot. The years have shown me that sometimes you just need to sit back and figure out what's driving the other person's behavior before reacting."

When reflecting on the situation, Miranda surmised that Lauren was feeling threatened about her friendship with Aileen. "Aileen had been raving about how great I was, but instead of bolstering me, her compliments were making Lauren jealous. I knew that over the years the two women colleagues had become good friends who even vacationed together with their spouses and children. Lauren didn't want me horning in on their thing. Once I recognized that her inappropriate behavior had stemmed from insecurity, I knew how to deal with her."

So what did Miranda do to reverse the situation?

"I made it clear to Lauren in small ways that I was on the team to get the job done and had no interest in being part of her social sphere with Aileen. It was such a simple tweak, but it worked. Before too long, Lauren started using me as a sounding board and relying on me for advice. And you know, despite tending to be insecure and a bit gruff, she was brilliant about strategy and incorporating out-of-the-box ideas into the project. I learned a lot working with her."

When you don't instantly hit it off with someone you work with or you are initially mistreated by a colleague, you will often discover it isn't your problem, but the other person's. Instead of escalating the situation or ignoring it, be big enough to shift your perspective and try a new approach, like Miranda did. Begin by asking yourself why your "tormentor" might be behaving the way she does. Make a list of her positive aspects and focus on those, instead of the negative ones. You might be surprised to find that beneath every "tormentor" lies a potentially great teacher or collaborator.

KNOW WHERE TO DRAW THE LINE BETWEEN SELF-IMPROVEMENT AND SELF-DESTRUCTION.

Sometimes your own worst critic is no one but yourself. Yes, it's good to be self-aware. Yes, it's good to be on top of things that you need to improve in yourself and your work. And yes, it's true that there is always something that you can do better. But it's all a matter of degree. You don't want to be so self-conscious about your imperfect areas—and who doesn't have them—that you become your own worst critic, to the point where it impacts your behavior and how others perceive you.

For example, forty-eight-year-old Judy carried a chip on her shoulder about not having a college degree that almost brought her down. A powerful executive who had risen through the ranks at a billion-dollar telecommunications firm and who now served as a trusted adviser to the CEO, Judy had never graduated from college. Rather than growing more confident as she rose through the ranks, she became more obsessed that her colleagues would find out about her educational status. In reality, however, few people knew, and those who did know didn't care. Although she had been working for the company for more than two decades, in Judy's eyes everything and everyone was suspect. She was always thinking that her colleagues were saying this, doing that, or treating her a certain way because of "it," when in fact "it" was the furthest thing from their minds. As a result, Judy misinterpreted all sorts of cues from her colleagues. When questioned about the most innocent thing, she launched into battle mode, responding in a very defensive, strident, and aggressive way that left people scratching their heads as to what they had done wrong. Judy had become so obsessed about lacking a college degree that she was missing a very significant problem facing her: colleagues were growing increasingly jealous of how the chairman turned to her more than to them. Now, this was something she *really* needed to be paying attention to.

After much coaching and coaxing, Judy took my advice and decided to get over it. First, she began to recognize that she was the only person who cared about her lack of a degree. A timely *Wall Street Journal* article, which noted that most CEOs of the biggest corporations had attended state universities or no-name private colleges rather than the Ivies, helped her see the light. Second, Judy made a list of everything she had accomplished during her career and looked at it at least once a day to remind herself of her achievements. Third, to avoid falling back into her old patterns of defensive behavior, she started responding to questions and concerns raised in meetings with unemotional language such as "That's an interesting perspective," and "Thanks for letting me know what's on your mind." She adopted new inner monologues, including "It's okay to disagree," and "I want them to understand why I think this."

Ultimately, Judy didn't just get over it, she got on with it. Acknowledging that she had always longed to finish college, she decided that as soon as her youngest son graduated from high school in two years, she would enroll in a local program for working adults to complete her college degree—this time, not for anyone else but herself.

STAY COOL IN THE HOT SEAT.

"I blew it so badly, Peggy. I totally lost my cool," said David, a thirty-six-year-old engineer who called on me for emergency assistance following his dismal performance at, ironically, his performance review.

Nine months previously, his new boss had arrived on the scene, and the two had been having trouble getting along ever since. "We're like oil and water," David remarked. Yet, through it all, he had managed to keep a level head. That is, until his performance review, when the boss announced that David's bonus would be the same as the year before and suggested three areas of much-needed improvement.

"One 'area of improvement' in particular got my goat because I felt it was so unfair, and soon I was yelling with indignation." Like a tidal wave gaining speed as it nears the shore, David found he couldn't stop himself. Before he knew it, more words tumbled out of his mouth, to the tune of "You're the worst boss I've ever had."

Throughout this chapter, I've covered various ways of dealing with being judged and criticized in various unexpected and informal situations. But, of course, being prepared is just as important when it comes to official performance reviews. Yet most people go into their review cold and clueless, or, as another client says, "on a wing and a prayer." As a result, people often look back at their review with regret. As David lamented later, after eventually losing his job, "It was truly a pivotal moment. If only I had learned sooner to stay cool in the hot seat."

No matter how difficult it is to conduct performance appraisals, it's no easier receiving one. In highly charged emotional situations, particularly when we feel judged or criticized, our listening skills break down. Our heart races. Our breath quickens. One way to sit in the hot seat with less dread and more dignity is to simply show up prepared.

David, for example, knew his relationship with the boss was nearing a boiling point, yet he had never even considered what might occur during the review—such as his boss saying something upsetting to him—and how he was going to handle it.

Remember, it's never too early to start planning for your next performance review by considering the following advice, most of which is equally useful when receiving informal feedback.

Be prepared. Begin by keeping a short daily log of interactions that pinpoints the who, what, when, where, how, and why of each of your significant accomplishments or mistakes. The best defense is a good offense.

Be as objective and unemotional as possible. Tell yourself, "I need to listen to this. It will help me grow personally and professionally." Stay present and tuned in to what you are hearing.

Listen without interruption. As you do so, jot down notes. Often when we get negative feedback, our brain freezes. We may stick on a certain word or phrase and not hear what else is being said. Jotting things down will keep you unstuck and help focus your attention on what the boss is saying from beginning to end. You can then look back at your notes later for reference and further discussion.

Ask yourself, "Is the feedback specific and action oriented?" People tend to give very general, amorphous feedback. Be ready to ask, "I'm not clear on what you want me to do differently," or "I'm not sure exactly what you're saying. Could you please be more specific?"

Follow up throughout the year. Don't wait until your next review to get more feedback from the boss. Set goals for improvement and then ask for regular input on how well you are achieving them.

Last, but not least, if you find yourself getting hot around the collar in the hot seat, diffuse the situation by saying this:

"May I have some time to think about this one, then talk with you about it later?"

Works like a charm.

Five

WHAT, ME POLITICAL?

- Learn the unspoken rules of your workplace.

- Two heads are better than one, so find a mentor.

- Don't let the fear of "sucking up" hold you back.

- When it comes to gossip, learn the art of deflection.

- Think long and hard about going over your boss's head.

- Manage your affairs: kiss with caution!

"But Peggy, I don't want to feel like I'm stuck in a daily boxing match at work," came a voice from the back of the room during a talk I was giving on handling office politics. "I just want to sit at my desk, do the job well, get an annual raise, and go home."

When it comes to office politics, many people share those exact same sentiments and find themselves falling into one of three camps: they deny that office politics even exist, they think it's possible to stay above the fray, or they claim that playing politics just isn't that important to them. Delusions like these have sent many a career into the danger zone. So if you are prone to thinking along similar lines—and you want to dramatically improve your chances for advancement and success—it's time to embrace the unspoken rules of your workplace.

Everyone starts out with a limited understanding of what constitutes office politics, but some people bumble along far too long without finding out the inner workings of their company. This is what I call the bubblehead syndrome—staying in a protective mental bubble while others around you make headway in the political sandbox. Then, one day, your job or project is on the chopping block. Suddenly, the bubble pops. You wake up and ask yourself, "What the heck is happening here?" And even once you realize that office politics really do exist, you might mistakenly think it's just about backstabbing and sharp elbows. While it's true that conflict is inevitable whenever people of widely varying backgrounds, agendas, and personalities work together, everyone isn't necessarily out to get each other. Much like the tongue-in-cheek definition of a dysfunctional family as any family with more than one member, you'll find office politics whenever there are two or more people in the same workplace jockeying for attention, position, and compensation.

Office politics are both inevitable and unavoidable. They are built into every job situation. Some people call it corporate gamesmanship, while others like to think about it more along the lines of organizational astuteness. Call it whatever you like—you will be affected by this phenomenon from day one, no matter what type of job you have or what industry you're in. So, whether you're going for a raise or a promotion, selling an idea or the vision of the company, promoting a pet project or doing any number of other things to get your job done, you not only need to get used to dealing with the politics at your workplace, you also need to get good at it.

Lessons in this chapter will bring into focus the underlying soft skills of organizational awareness, influence through alliances, mentorships, reaching out to senior management, learning the art of deflection when it comes to gossip, resolving conflicts with your boss, and handling yourself with dignity when a professional relationship turns personal.

LEARN THE UNSPOKEN RULES OF YOUR WORKPLACE.

How do power and influence manifest in your department? Which players carry the most weight? Who gets along with whom? How are decisions made? Where are the gaps between policy and practice? What are the company customs from wardrobe expectations to holiday traditions? Don't know the answers to these questions? Then you better find them out soon, because the first unspoken rule of office politics is to become a keen observer of the unique personality and character of your workplace. Some people refer to this unofficial company culture as the shadow organization, which is what *really* determines the protocol at your workplace for how things are done and who gets ahead. I asked a few people whom I admire for their political savvy to share their encounters with the shadow side of where they work. Here's a sampling of their responses.

- *Although the office officially opens at nine o'clock, anyone who wants to get the attention of the president—who by the way, arrives at 5:30 a.m. daily—should be at work no later than 8:00 a.m.*

- *The best place to engage in conversation with our CEO is on the golf course, on Sundays, no less.*

- *Nothing will ever happen unless Marcia says yes. She will never say yes unless she gets the nod from her boss, Jerry. And for Jerry, it's always about the bottom line. If he doesn't see the dollars making sense, don't waste your breath.*

- *Although no one pays much attention to Roberta in research, she's actually a close confidante of the CEO. They went to college together, and she always has the pulse on what he's thinking and what's coming down the pike.*

- *If you need action on something, go to Zach's assistant Mary Anne. She can make anything happen.*

- *Don't propose an idea unless you can measure some type of return in sixteen months. Why sixteen months? Only the gods know, but it's one of Byron's golden rules, and everyone lives by it.*

- *Zoey always sits in the third chair from the right in the conference room. Her spot is hallowed ground. So, if you want to be on her good side, don't even think of sitting there.*

- *Before you try to talk to Margaret, make an appointment. She isn't the type of person you can just drop in to see. Also, she doesn't do "chitchat," so get to the point, get her feedback, and get out.*

- *Our company is full of eco-fanatics. If you pull into the parking lot in a Hummer—or even an ordinary gas-guzzling SUV—it's unlikely you'll be well regarded by anyone.*

- *Don't bother complaining about Wes. He's been here forever. His grandfather and the president's grandfather were old pals. They'll never get rid of him. The key is to go around him as much as you can.*

Whenever you are new to a job or a position, turn on your company culture radar. Invest some time and energy in absorbing the politics of the environment before getting too involved or deciding where to plant yourself down. The more you observe, listen, and ask questions in the early days, the sooner you'll discover who is really driving the train, how to best fit in, and what it will take to become more than just another passenger. Ultimately, the degree to which you master the unspoken rules of your workplace determines the degree of success you will experience in any given job situation.

TWO HEADS ARE BETTER THAN ONE, SO FIND A MENTOR.

"Who's your advocate?" I asked Yvonne, a twenty-eight-year-old sales executive who had just told me her idea for expanding the company's professional development initiative to help women develop their leadership potential.

Looking befuddled, she responded, "I didn't know I was supposed to have one."

One of the most critical steps you can take in the arena of office politics is to form an alliance with a mentor, someone who will put you under his or her wing and guide you. A good mentor can champion your ideas, help you meet the "right people," and help you lay the foundation for building a network of support and influence so that you can more easily navigate the shadow organization.

For example, Yvonne's mentor—whom she searched for and found after our conversation—suggested building strong ties with the company's marketing department, since it was always on the lookout for ideas that would showcase the firm's progressive position on women's leadership and diversity issues. She also advised Yvonne to build support for her initiative over time by meeting informally with a number of the key players in the organization to gain their input and buy-in before taking things any further.

Gordon, who couldn't be "bothered with things like finding mentors," was less fortunate. The first time I met him, he was completely devastated by having been overlooked for a promotion. I asked him a few questions and, within minutes, realized what the problem was: he hadn't even bothered to run the race. A good mentor, had he bothered to have one, would have forewarned him that there would be competition for the coveted position and would have advised him on who to talk to regarding his interest long before the formal hiring process even began. Apparently, what had happened instead is that Gordon sat idly by, uncomfortable about letting his intentions be known because, "that would seem too political." Meanwhile, his opponent was greasing the wheels and letting everyone on the selection committee know about his ambitions, qualifications, and ideas for the running the department, were they to choose him.

Wendy got blindsided as well, not by a peer, but by her own boss. As she said, "I never dreamed that when I got transferred to Europe that my boss—the guy who had hired me—would feel so threatened and spend the next two years trying to get me fired." Now, looking back nearly two decades later with much more experience under her belt, Wendy said that it all boiled down to her having been totally clueless and unprotected politically. "Had I been smarter, I would have taken the time to observe the landscape when I first arrived and chart out the key alliances I needed to build. Having been with the company in the States for several years, I didn't recognize the importance of developing a mentoring relationship with someone within the European organization."

So how do you find a mentor? Sometimes mentoring relationships occur naturally. You might connect with a boss or the person who first introduced you to the company. Other times, you find a mentor through the firm's formal mentoring program (if it has one), although this option isn't always ideal. Sometimes the person assigned to you is just not the right fit.

The last thing you want to do is learn the hard way, like Gordon and Wendy did, or to slip up and choose a charmer who gets you to confide but isn't looking out for your best interests. So here are some guidelines for choosing a mentor.

The person should . . .

. . . have stature in the organization—people who have stature usually know how to play the game well.

. . . be experienced with the company and ideally your department.

. . . already have proven themselves to be an advocate for you or others.

. . . be someone others hold in high regard and have nice things to say about (think twice about choosing a mentor who seems great, but about whom others say bad things behind their back).

. . . have given you reason to think you can trust them.

After coming up with your list of people with terrific qualifications, you'll most likely be wondering, "Why would someone like that want to help out someone like me?"

You'll be surprised to hear that people—no matter how high up the ladder they might be—are generally flattered when someone asks them to be their mentor. When it's time for you to approach the candidate, be sure to let him know why you've singled him out (you've been impressed with his insight and perceptiveness at company meetings, so-and-so recommended him, etc.) and how much you would appreciate his advice on an ongoing basis. If he is interested, discuss potential time commitments and your respective expectations for the relationship. If he turns you down, try the next person on your list.

Unless you already have a second set of brains on tap for coaching and guidance, it's time to make your list and start asking.

DON'T LET THE FEAR OF "SUCKING UP" HOLD YOU BACK.

"I didn't want to appear that I was 'sucking up,'" said thirty-seven-year-old Marcus, a systems analyst, explaining to me why he had switched place cards with his colleague at the dinner table at the conference. By doing so, he had forgone the opportunity to sit next to the senior vice president of research and development, someone he really needed to get to know.

I couldn't believe my ears. Well, maybe I could. This wasn't the first time I'd witnessed an opportunity fly right past because someone feared looking like a suck-up. You know who I mean, right? I'm talking about those people who will go to any length to ingratiate themselves with the higher-ups and are often observed in the act of . . .

> . . . hanging on to and agreeing with everything they say.

> . . . responding to their beck and call—not unlike a lapdog.

> . . . offering incessant, and often undeserved, compliments.

> . . . laughing at their jokes, even when they're not funny.

Okay, I admit it. These people make me want to gag, too. But what you've got to learn—and what successful players already know—is that forging a good relationship with superiors is always smart business and that not getting to know them is always a bad idea.

Marcus, however, had taken his fear of being seen as a suck-up to the point of ridiculousness by resisting the opportunity of sitting next to someone influential just to avoid the perception of playing politics. Luckily, he self-corrected by our next session. When we discussed what had happened that evening, Marcus shared his reflections. "You know, Peggy, I've always thought of myself as above the fray. I don't consider myself political and don't want to be seen that way. Sure, I would say hello to the company president when I saw him in passing, but I never really engaged with him like many of my colleagues did. So while walking back to my room after dinner that night, I replayed the evening in my mind. 'What jerks, what suck-ups, my colleagues are,' I had thought to myself. 'You won't see me kissing up to anyone to get ahead.' But then later, as I was reading over some notes from our last coaching session, it suddenly hit me how wrong I had been. Who did I really hurt by being a political priss and thinking of myself as above the fray? Only myself! I had passed up a golden opportunity to make myself known to the VP. How stupid was that?"

It's absolutely essential that you actively seek out informal opportunities to engage with senior executives in your company. Does that mean that you magically show up uninvited where the mighty congregate? Of course not! If you're the least bit obvious in your intentions, you've blown it. The key is to work your way in slowly and discreetly. For example, one woman I know decided to take up golf, once she noticed that the local club was where many of the company's executives gathered to conduct business late in the afternoon. She was already athletic and picked the game up in no time. When the warmer months rolled around, she entered a mixed-gender tournament at the club and, in the course of play, wowed a couple of the men from her office. Word quickly got around in the corporate suite that she was a very good golfer and soon she was invited to fill in for someone who was away on business, then asked to be a regular. She swears that connecting to the higher-ups through golf has done more for her career than any single thing she's done since graduating from college.

Golf aside, do some research on the people in your own firm who are important to your advancement. Often the company Web site or internal newsletter is a good place to start looking for common connections, be it through a commitment to a cause, sports, or a shared alumni affiliation.

WHEN IT COMES TO GOSSIP, LEARN THE ART OF DEFLECTION.

"Go read *People* magazine, or the *National Enquirer,* or take a cold shower."

This isn't the kind of advice you might expect to hear from a senior executive, yet those are exactly the words of wisdom one manager I know recently gave her up-and-comers about getting embroiled in office gossip. "Instead of turning against your colleagues, get your gossip fix reading the tabloids," she tells them.

I know you've probably heard the whole song and dance when it comes to gossip at the office: It's distracting, it's counterproductive, and it's bad for business. Indeed, there's a reason why even ancient religious law advises against repeating things about others (even when true!) unless it's absolutely imperative that the information be conveyed. Judaism recognizes the power of speech to harm and that gossiping, as one rabbi suggested, can be the equivalent of taking a down pillow, cutting it open, and scattering the feathers to the winds. Just as it is impossible to reclaim each and every feather, it's impossible to reclaim each and every word. If you spill negative words about someone who is not present to defend himself, the damage caused cannot always be undone or stopped from spreading—it's like thousands of tiny feathers indiscriminately blowing in the wind.

Despite the ill effects of gossiping, however, no workplace is immune to it. Instead, many people find gossip irresistible on both the receiving and giving ends. I'm sure you've heard all the explanations for why people gossip, such as that they are insecure and trying to build themselves up by tearing someone else down. Or that it's a form of entertainment in an otherwise boring day. Social anthropologists might tell you that it's simply part of human nature.

Fair enough. But here's another reason that really goes to the heart of the matter: Gossip is a way for people to bond and feel like they are part of the inner circle, that they are "in the know." It makes them feel special, particularly when they have a hot tidbit to share that no one has heard yet. We start treating the news as a commodity, an asset that can raise our value and be traded on at the office. Voilà, it makes us more of a player.

Trust me, though, when I say this is not the kind of politics that's ultimately career-elevating. Close your eyes. Think for a second about the CGO (chief gossip officer) at your own workplace. Every company seems to have one—the busybody who always has the goods on everyone. Or maybe you're lucky enough to have several of these folks in your office. If that's the case, I doubt thinking about them makes a smile spread across your face.

While most of us don't aspire to the title of CGO, we all struggle with how best to handle ourselves when confronted with gossip. The best advice to follow is something your mom probably already told you: don't say anything behind someone's back that you wouldn't say to their face. Yes, it's always best to take the high ground, or as a client of mine says, "Clamp it shut!"

So the next time your coworkers try drawing you into a gossip fest by asking for your opinion, practice the art of deflection to avoid participation without coming across with a holier-than-thou attitude. For example, when someone says, "Don't you think your boss Patricia blew it? She seems really distracted lately," here are a few ways in which you can respond:

- "Have you shared your thoughts with Patricia?"

- "I don't really know about that."

- "Why not talk to her about your concerns?"

- "Patricia's been a great boss for me."

One of the key ways to practice the art of deflection is to put the onus of resolving the issue raised by the gossiper back on them and stay positive, rather than joining in with your own take on the matter.

THINK LONG AND HARD ABOUT GOING OVER YOUR BOSS'S HEAD.

Camille believed she had finally outfoxed the fox, her boss.

While hobnobbing with some of the company's senior executives at an industry trade show, she pulled aside her boss's supervisor to give him a blow-by-blow account of her boss's incompetence on both the last product launch and the upcoming one. As she later recalled, it was as though she couldn't stop herself once she got started. Eleven months of pent-up frustration from working for the dimwit came spilling out. Plus, having gotten to know her boss's boss, the district manager, fairly well during the course of working for the firm, she reasoned he would keep this between themselves. What Camille didn't realize at the time of her venting session were three critical things: (1) the conversation would not be kept in confidence, (2) she was committing political suicide, and (3) her boss would outwit her in the end.

You see, in order for the district manager to address the issue, he had to tell Camille's boss who had brought it to his attention in the first place. This necessitated revealing the clandestine discussion at the trade show. At the end of the day, Camille had made things worse—much worse than she had ever anticipated. Relations with her boss were already strained, but now they headed even farther south. He no longer trusted her at all, and, quite frankly, Camille had raised the district manager's eyebrow due to the way she had handled the situation. He wondered whether she would perform the same "end run" on him someday, were she to be promoted.

Think back for a second: has someone ever gone over your head? How did it feel? If you're like most humans, it probably made you very uncomfortable and distrustful of the person. And that's exactly how Camille's boss felt. From then on, he conveniently overlooked her during important discussions. Whenever opportunities for advancement came up, he completely shut her out. While Camille worked hard to rebuild some semblance of a professional relationship, it wasn't possible, and she eventually left the company.

Are you thinking of going over your boss's head? As a rule of thumb, don't! Forget about circumventing the chain of command unless there are extreme circumstances, such as when your boss . . .

. . . engages in illegal activity, such as stealing from the company.

. . . hides having a serious physical or mental illness or drug addiction.

. . . exposes the company to a lawsuit through sexual harassment or some other unlawful action.

If your company has policies on what do in situations like these, find out what they are and follow them. If it does not, and you think that going to your boss first is inadvisable or even potentially dangerous, be sure to have your facts straight before reaching out to the human resources manager or your boss's supervisor. Depending on the situation, you might consider seeking private legal counsel before you proceed. Be careful to keep all information confidential, while at the same time saving e-mails and documenting conversations with whomever you approach for assistance.

For less-extreme matters, it's always best to first discuss the grievance with your boss. If he or she continues to ignore your concern or has little interest in resolving the situation, don't be afraid to say, "I'm frustrated with our progress on this. Do you have any other ideas we can try? Perhaps we can set a timeline for resolving our differences."

If you find that you are still at an impasse after numerous discussions and you've exhausted all options, then let your boss know that you intend to take the matter up with another person, be it someone in human resources or your boss's supervisor. For example, you could say, "We've talked about this a lot already and we can't seem to come to any resolution. So I feel I need to talk to Marvin in HR about this. Would you like to go with me to discuss this with him? I'm telling you about my plans beforehand, because I don't want to go behind your back."

Remember, if you do speak with someone else about your boss, stay clear of character assassination and stick to the issues or behaviors that are problematic and at the center of your conflict. Otherwise, your complaint will sound like sour grapes and you'll come off as a whiner, rather than someone who is trying to solve a problem.

In any case, recognize that your relationship with your boss will probably be changed forever once you go over his or her head—even if you fully disclose your intentions before taking the leap. That's because for many managers, loyalty trumps everything.

MANAGE YOUR AFFAIRS: KISS WITH CAUTION!

Janet was caught off guard. Her counterpart, the manager of another department, was on the phone demanding an answer. "Why are you spreading rumors about Sally and me?"

As the HR director, Janet couldn't believe what she was hearing. "Excuse me," she said, "First of all, I haven't spread any rumors about Sally and you—so, quite honestly, I really object to you accusing me of that. Second, and even more important, your entire team was in my office last week telling me that they think you are having an affair with Sally, which is making them all feel very uncomfortable." Several people from his team said they had seen them together acting very cozy. "And if that's the case," Janet told him, "you should move Sally immediately to another group. After all, she does report to you!"

A peer-to-peer romance was one thing in Janet's book, but one between an employee and a supervisor was an entirely different matter. Such a relationship could create resentment and morale issues for the other employees, undermine the credibility of management decisions, and give rise to claims of sexual harassment.

Canoodling in the copy room? PDAs (public displays of affection) in the elevator? Love e-mails gone astray? Does this sound like the plot of the latest soap opera or grade-B movie? Well, it's probably already playing at a workplace near you. While once considered taboo, office romance has come out of the closet. People are now finding Cupid at work in record numbers for the simple reason that—for better or worse—more and more of our time is spent at work.

According to an office romance survey by CareerBuilder, 43 percent of the U.S. workforce reports having dated a coworker. Thirty-four percent of those who coupled up with a fellow employee said they ended up marrying that person. One-in-ten respondents said they currently have their eye on someone at the office for dating in the near future. Thirty-four percent of workers said they had to keep their relationship with a colleague a secret. Twenty-two percent admitted having dated a colleague who was married, and 27 percent went out with someone who holds a higher position than they do within their organization. And, bringing us back to Sally, 14 percent have dated their boss.

Providing further evidence of a shift in attitude about office romance, Southwest Airlines has openly publicized the fact that it employs more than a thousand married couples. However, if you think what you do on your own time is "none of the company's business," think again. While 70 percent of firms have no written dating policies in place, more and more are developing them, particularly when it concerns a supervisor and a direct report. The following language is an example of the type of clause you might find in the employee handbook of a corporation having such a policy:

The manager is required to disclose to the Human Resources Director any relationship that he or she becomes aware of between a supervisor and a subordinate that is of a romantic or sexual nature. The Human Resources Director will determine at his or her discretion whether or not to transfer one or both of the employees involved. If a transfer is required but not available or is not accepted by the employee(s), then one or both of them may be terminated.

There's probably no stopping nature running its course, but when it comes to office romance, proceed with caution and consider what you are getting into. Think about how your actions might be perceived and the possible ramifications in your career. The effects it will have on the political landscape depend largely on how you and your companion handle yourselves and the particular situation. For example, if your partner works in an entirely different department or for a company subsidiary, getting together may have little bearing at all. Conversely, if you are dating your boss's boss, the implications will undoubtedly be considerable.

In addition, keep this in mind if you have the hots for someone at work: even if you've checked out that your company policy allows it or takes a "don't ask, don't tell" approach, a "never" policy might be a good idea, especially when it's someone you are working over or under. If you decide to go ahead, then consider the following guidelines:

- Adopt a policy of no canoodling or PDAs at work. There's nothing worse than sitting at a table trying to have a business discussion when "two people are going gaga over each other," as one of my clients so aptly put it. It's extremely important to always maintain a sense of decorum and professionalism. For example, one couple I know stops holding hands just as soon as they get out of the car in the company parking lot. Another workplace couple decided it's best to commute separately to work.

- Agree ahead of time about how to handle the inevitable conflicts that will come up both inside and outside of the office. If you have a fight at breakfast, for example, you need to leave that emotional baggage outside the office door. For disagreements that happen at work, refrain from making personal comments in front of others.

- Consider the "what ifs:" What if one gets promoted and the other doesn't? What if the company goes under? Can you both afford to lose jobs at the same time? What if the romance doesn't work out? Be sure to have an exit strategy that works for both of you.

Relationships are a critical component of office politics. Given that one of the strongest and most intense connections you can form is a romantic one, you better be prepared before sharing that first embrace with someone from the office.

Six

BRANDING AND BRAGGING

- Think of yourself as a cereal brand.

- Turn your accomplishments into a story.

- Tooting your own horn isn't just for performance reviews.

- You're only as good as your last movie, so keep your brags fresh.

- Put the right words in their mouths.

- Keep your visibility when you're not face-to-face.

- Stop credit thieves in their tracks.

Do you think branding is just for cows and that *brag* is a four-letter word? Like a horse and carriage, branding and bragging go hand in hand. Your brand is the image that comes to people's minds when they think about you, whereas bragging (the right way, of course!) is one of the most powerful tools for delivering the message behind your brand. When it comes to self-promotion, many of us wince and then make excuses. We can't imagine ourselves as products competing for shelf space. We think that tooting our own horn is largely limited to those special occasions like job interviews or performance reviews. Or, more likely, we get stuck in the "myth mire"—those countless things we were told growing up that keep us from ever singing our own praises, like "Hard work speaks for itself." And "Nice girls don't brag." Or one of my all-time favorites, "Someone else will always be better than you, so don't think you're so great."

A client of mine, Cheryl, works for a very large engineering company. While meeting with all of the division managers in her boss's office, she overheard one of the other division heads saying to the boss, "I'm really delighted that my group met the deadline for those financials in January. They really hit it on target!" After that meeting, Cheryl relayed her reaction to me, "Peggy, I thought to myself, 'She's such a blowhard. My department has done that for thirteen months in a row and I've never mentioned it to anyone. Who cares if she pulled it off just once?' But as soon as that thought crossed my mind, what you've been telling me in our sessions about bragging finally clicked and I had my aha moment: Our boss cares, that's who! I realized then that I should have been doing the exact same thing myself for the last thirteen months."

The art of branding and bragging is all about bringing a soft touch to the soft skill of self-promotion. This is how you stand out from the crowd and keep your accomplishments in your boss's mind when it comes to raises, promotions, and succession planning, or when your company is trying to decide who stays and who goes during mergers, management shifts, and downsizing. It doesn't matter whether you're seeking advancement in your current position, ready to change an established career, or just starting out—you have to be ever mindful of cultivating your own personal brand and promoting it.

Next up, we'll be covering some of the most important components of soft skills associated with self-promotion, including identifying and building your brand, managing how people perceive you, learning the art of storytelling to promote yourself, always staying relevant, influencing others in spreading your message, and speaking up when your good deeds get hijacked by others. Hopefully, by the end of this chapter, you'll be more comfortable doing what your parents probably told you not to: brag!

THINK OF YOURSELF AS A CEREAL BRAND.

So what do all the ready-to-eat cereal brands lining your supermarket aisle have to do with you being a standout at work?

Close your eyes for a second and think of the brand name Wheaties. What comes to mind? The breakfast of champions, of course. The image of a healthy and nutritious cereal that's eaten by fit and athletic types like Michael Jordan, Tiger Woods, and Olympic gold medalists.

If you were to do the same for Cheerios, you'd probably conjure up thoughts of whole-grain oats that are good-tasting and good for you. It's a healthy, tried-and-true cereal that you can feed to your kids—even toddlers—without feeling guilty. Translation: I completely trust this brand for my family.

What's prompting you to conjure those positive images and associations? Branding! We all know that product branding is designed to create an emotional response in consumers. Well, it turns out that many of the same strategies companies use successfully with their products apply equally well to branding yourself.

In today's competitive environment, self-branding is an essential element of establishing your reputation in the business world and distinguishing yourself from the pack. It's how you can convey your core values, highlight your talents, and present your passion to bosses, colleagues, and clients. For certain, everyone around you is forming an opinion about your brand each and every day. So think carefully about what you want them to be feeling and thinking about Brand You.

Many years ago, around the time I was first contemplating the concept of personal branding, I coached someone who worked in marketing. If anyone really knew about branding, it would be this woman. During the course of her career, she had been responsible for overseeing a number of brands in one of the most competitive consumer packaged goods categories—the cereal aisle (back to Wheaties and Cheerios again). During hours of discussions with my client, the consumer products maven, I became even more convinced that while not everything done in the branding of consumer products applies to people, most of the basic principles are the same. The difference is that instead of highlighting cereals or baby food and shampoo or athletic shoes, the product is *you*.

For instance, your brand is a promise—implied or explicit—of the value you offer, what you bring to the table. Your brand— whether carefully crafted or left to chance—determines the image that will pop to mind when others are thinking about you. Unlike the cereal brands, however, you won't have a marketing department or advertising budget for your campaign and will need to take a do-it-yourself approach.

The first step in creating brand awareness is to determine what your brand is by answering the following questions:

- What are three of your core values (i.e., dependability, creativity, honesty, etc.)?

- What are five key talents and characteristics that best reflect your professional expertise (i.e., financial whiz, many years in the field, a large network in the industry, etc.)?

- What are five communication or personality characteristics that you consider to be your strengths?

- Who is currently aware of your brand and how would they describe it?

- How would you like your brand to be described?

- What are the gaps between your current brand image and what you would like it to be?

- What specifically can you do to alleviate or eliminate these gaps?

The next step is to write down how you think your brand is perceived today. Then compose a clear and powerful written statement of ten words or less describing how you would like your brand to be perceived. Here are some examples.

- HR director: *Develops the company's top leaders for tomorrow's challenges.*

- Managing director of an investment bank: *Knows what it takes to run a first-class M & A practice.* (M & A means mergers and acquisitions.)

- Headhunter: *Finds the right people for the right job at the right time.*

- Editorial assistant at a publishing company: *Gets the job done no matter what it takes.*

- Associate at a recycling firm: *Straight shooter, always tells it like it is.*

- Senior partner at an executive consulting firm: *Builds business in the C suites (CEOs, CFOs, COOs, CIOs).*

- Owner of an executive development firm: *Empowers women for success in their professional and personal lives.*

Once you've identified how others perceive you in the present and how you want them to think about you in the future, the next step is to create exposure and self-promotion opportunities for getting your message out. Think to yourself: In what situations should my brand be more evident (i.e., client pitches, conversations with senior management, meetings, etc.)? Use some or all of the following suggestions for building relationships with key internal and external contacts to promote Brand You to target audiences:

- Strengthen relationships with colleagues in your department or others with whom you work closely.

- Find ways to meet people in the company who work outside of your area.

- Keep your boss and colleagues apprised of your projects at meetings and through e-mails or voice mails.

- Introduce yourself to the higher-ups within your department or the organization.

- Get involved in one of your company's committees.

- Identify five key players that you think should know you better and take them to coffee or lunch.

- Get involved in events that are planned for clients.

- Attend industry-related conferences.

- Mentor a junior associate.

My final advice for getting your brand out is to learn how to talk about yourself and your accomplishments without turning off those you're trying to impress. Read on and I'll show you how.

TURN YOUR ACCOMPLISHMENTS INTO A STORY.

"What makes you memorable?"

I posed that question to Colleen, a forty-two-year-old project manager for a telecommunications firm. She was completely sold on the concept of personal branding. Now it was time to give her brand a voice.

Right away, Colleen launched into a litany of "I" statements, delivered in a monotone voice: "I went to Harvard. I got my master's in English. I got a job in telecommunications with a wireless carrier. In 2000, I got promoted to the head of project management in corporate services."

Quite frankly, I can't remember what else Colleen said because by the time she was finished, I was numb.

There are good ways and not-so-good ways to self-promote. We're all familiar with bad bragging: talking nonstop, interrupting, exaggerating, lying, stealing credit, name-dropping, and so on. In addition, there's the intolerable laundry list that goes like "I did this, and then I did that, and then I also did this other thing before I went on to do the next thing, and blah, blah, blah." Believe me, there's nothing better for making you come off as both boring and self-aggrandizing than rattling off a laundry list of past accomplishments.

On the other hand, good bragging converts all those "I" statements into conversational and storylike chunks, to be delivered with the kind of enthusiasm with which you would tell a friend about an exciting trip you've just returned from. I call these conversation chunks bragologues, a word I coined to evoke a combo platter of monologue meets brag.

Bragologues are interesting to listen to and are powerful tools that get people to think about you in just the ways you want. They are woven together with a few memorable or impressive nuggets of information called brag bites. These could be pieces of relevant facts, such as clients that you're working with, how long you've been in the industry, or a project you've recently completed.

Some people associate bragologues with the fifteen-second elevator pitch. You bump into the chairman in the elevator. Quick, what do you say? You have just fifteen seconds to introduce yourself and grab his attention. Bragologues are equally useful at cocktail parties, at industry conferences, on airplanes, or whenever someone asks you what you do for a living. They also come in handy when you're giving a presentation and no one is assigned to introduce you to the audience.

Bragologues can best be explained through real-life examples, so here are a few.

Noah, what are you most proud of?

Bad Bragging: "I'm a great sales manager because I'm good with people. At the end of the month, I always get the top numbers."

Good Bragging: "You know, when I was first hired as sales manager, I had no idea what a great fit it would be for my skills and personality. The job encompasses everything that I love and do well such as my organizational skills, an ability to bring out the best in people, and years of hands-on sales experience, which helps me really understand what my team is going through."

Stephanie, tell me what you do for work and how you got into the business?

Bad Bragging: "I work for a life insurance company. For those of you who know life insurance, it tends to be a very conservative business, but I'm in the IT department and I'm actually responsible for introducing new technologies to the company."

Good Bragging: "I've been working for more than ten years at a major life insurance company where I began in IT at the ground level, literally in the basement of the building at the help desk. Because of my curiosity about the business and my drive, I moved from the help desk to the field, and then something new came up. It was the Internet. Of course, since I work in the conservative life insurance industry, everyone at my company thought this was going to be a fad that would soon blow over. But I was certain it wouldn't, and was able to convince my boss that there was an opportunity there. We didn't start selling insurance on the Internet—at least not then—but we developed an early online presence by starting a company Web site. Of course, nowadays our customers can do everything at our Web site, from getting a quote to paying their bill."

Ethan, how did you get into banking?

Bad bragging: "I got my first job through a friend of a friend."

Good bragging: "My gosh! You know, this year I am celebrating my twentieth year in banking, and if someone had told me or my parents that I would end up in this industry, we would have laughed, because I was someone who couldn't even balance my checkbook! But something clicked for me while I was getting my MBA that made me excited about going into banking after graduation. And now I'm working with high-net-worth individuals with assets ranging from five million dollars to twenty million dollars."

Carla, I heard through the grapevine you got a promotion. Congratulations!

Bad Bragging: "Yes, I'm now chief of staff to the president of my organization [a well-known international nonprofit]."

Good Bragging: "I guess we haven't spoken since my promotion to chief of staff to the president of [name of the nonprofit]. While I've worked closely with her for the last three years, I'm now officially her right-hand person. Current projects we are working on include expanding both the major donor campaign and the board of directors. We'll also be looking at the overall organization as a whole to see what improvements are needed. One of the new parts of my job that I'm enjoying most is the travel. I've just returned from a fact-finding mission to Vietnam, where we're involved in a project to eradicate AIDS. It was an incredible trip, and I'm thrilled to be part of the organization in this new position."

The goal is to have a variety of brag bites that you can string together into a fresh and relevant bragologue on a moment's notice. What you *don't* want to have are bragologues-in-a-can. You know, the same old thing you say over and over whenever you're asked, "So, what do you do?" If you're growing bored with your answer, it's certain to come across as even more boring to the person you're talking to. That's why it's good to keep a notebook of your brag bites and add to it frequently. This way, your bragologues won't go stale.

Once people reframe their stories and accomplishments into entertaining and conversational stories, their bad bragging days are over.

TOOTING YOUR OWN HORN ISN'T JUST FOR PERFORMANCE REVIEWS.

"I really blew it, Peggy," said Maya, a twenty-nine-year-old aerospace engineer. During the last couple of months, Maya, a highly reluctant tooter, had been getting ready for her upcoming performance review, where she had planned to pitch herself for a substantial salary increase.

"How could that be? You prepared and practiced a lot for that performance review," I responded, perplexed that it could have gone so poorly.

"No, I'm not talking about that—the performance review went great and it looks like I am going to get at least eighty percent of the raise I asked for," she responded. "Where I blew it was during a chance meeting with the president of the company just a day later!"

Apparently, on the heels of her performance review and with only three hours' notice, Maya was invited to replace her boss—who was delayed returning from a business trip to Denver due to inclement weather—at a fund-raising luncheon, where the company was sponsoring a table. "The truth is," Maya told me, "I don't think he would have ever even thought of asking me, but I had come off so strong in that review, reminding him of all my accomplishments and milestones, that I think he began to see me differently."

At the luncheon, however, Maya wasn't the least bit prepared for the CEO of her multibillion-dollar firm taking the seat right across from her. "I never imagined he would be there to begin with, but there he was. He seemed very approachable, even leaned over the table to shake my hand and warmly introduced himself. Later, when he asked me how my department was doing, I was tongue-tied and babbled on about something really lame. I really couldn't think of anything to say about myself except for that speech I'd prepared to persuade my boss on why I deserved a raise. Of course, that wasn't appropriate for repeating to the CEO! Unfortunately, I just didn't have anything else up my sleeve and completely missed the opportunity to impress him."

Earlier, I mentioned how important it is to learn how to handle critics because everyone is being judged all the time. In the same vein, when it comes to learning how to self-promote effectively, you need to be ready 24/7 anytime, anywhere, for anyone. The opportunities are going to come your way when you least expect them, from elevator "flybys" to your nephew's bar mitzvah. You never know who you will meet at a conference, a party, in the line at the grocery store, or while waiting for an airplane.

Like a good scout, be prepared not just for those scheduled situations, but also for those times that you weren't expecting to be "on." Sit down at your computer or grab a notebook—right now would be a good time—and create what I call your brag bag, a running tab of all the information about your best self that can be easily accessed when you need it: accomplishments, passions, and interests. Get specific; capture the colorful details that describe who you are both personally and professionally. Some people update their brag bags daily so they won't forget. At a minimum, I recommend you do it once a week, since it's hard to remember all the great things that happen if you wait too long to write them down. Also, when you capture things in writing, they'll more easily stick in your mind. Once you've put them down, read your brag bites out loud several times until you can rattle them off the tip of your tongue without even thinking.

While you do want to be *ready* 24/7, that doesn't mean you brag 24/7. Please use discretion. For example, a funeral is hardly the appropriate place to launch into your story. Similarly, walking into your boss's office during a time of crisis when he or she is distracted would definitely not be a good time for bragging.

YOU'RE ONLY AS GOOD AS YOUR LAST MOVIE, SO KEEP YOUR BRAGS FRESH.

Who hasn't been at a party where you've tried desperately to avoid that certain someone who talks about her same old accomplishment over and over again like a broken record? A friend of mine recently told me about a guy she calls Stanford, who is part of her extended social circle. "You can't ever have a conversation without him reminding you that he went to Stanford University. It's unbelievable how he always manages to bring it up. Every time I hear him go on and on and on about his alma mater, I want to say, 'Stop! I know you're a smart guy. I know you went to Stanford. You don't have to tell me yet again. Got anything else to talk about that you have done with your life in the last twenty years?'"

One of my clients learned firsthand how stale brags can come back to bite you in a rather harsh way. Having previously worked for a premier Wall Street investment bank for nearly two decades, he had just launched his own private equity firm. While recently meeting with a prospective client to give her his "spiel," as he called it (when someone calls it that you know it's a bad sign), he repeatedly relayed his prior experience with this top Wall Street bank. Finally, the woman interrupted, saying, "Russ, I am going to stop you right there. Because we've been friends for so many years, I'm going to give you some advice. First of all, you were half an hour late. Maybe you got away with that when working at your prestigious bank, but don't do that again to me or anybody else. Frankly, it's rude, and I'm now going to be late for my next appointment. Second, I need to tell you that no one cares as much as you do about your past with your previous firm. So, yes, while it's okay to drop it in to demonstrate your experience, don't keep mentioning it—it's over, done. People want to know what you are up to now and why they should be doing business with you." My client relayed this story to me with his head buried in his hands, deadly embarrassed and horrified that anything he had said to his friend and potential client would ever elicit such a response.

It's important that you keep your brags fresh. Everyone is more interested in what you're up to now. Just as in Hollywood, what matters most is not the movie you made twenty years ago, ten years ago, or even just a couple of years ago, it's the one you made most recently that counts. You need to be constantly refueling your brag campaign to reflect changes in your circumstances and audience. What worked yesterday may no longer work today, depending on the players and the circumstances. Measure your success in tangible and specific outcomes, such as receiving positive feedback from your boss or client, landing that next big project, or nabbing a giant bonus. These are some of the indicators that your self-promotion efforts are paying off. In any case, track your results. As time goes on, you may find yourself becoming less vigilant about promoting yourself and your brand, especially if you've had success with many of your goals. But just remember, your brand follows you wherever you go—be sure it's the *you* that you intend for everyone to know.

PUT THE RIGHT WORDS IN THEIR MOUTHS.

What's worse: Listening to someone's stale brags about themselves, about someone else, or about *you?*

I recently offered to put together a meeting to introduce a writer friend to some clients of mine—four partners in a well-established marketing and public relations firm who were looking for a freelancer. I thought I had prepared for everything—from a restaurant close to everyone's office to a prelunch e-mail outlining three things to discuss. The one thing I failed to plan was a bragologue about my friend. So when my introduction of her tumbled out, it was less than stellar. I tangled the details of my friend's job experience so badly that by the time I was done, she had worked for seventy-nine years. Also, I was uncertain about her current projects and so incorrectly placed her on an assignment she completed more than three months ago.

My friend graciously transitioned into telling her story without so much as a raised eyebrow or dirty look. Fortunately, after an hour and a half of effective damage control, the partners asked her for a follow-up meeting the next week. As I was driving home, although relieved that things had ended well, I couldn't help but reflect back on the situation. I realized my mistakes: I should have checked in with my friend prior to the meeting (and not just as we were walking to the table). I should have written down her information and turned it into a bragologue. And I should have practiced several times out loud, paraphrasing the facts until they felt comfortable rolling off my tongue. Okay, so that's where I goofed. However, as much as I blamed myself, my friend was equally culpable. After all, it was her big chance to sell herself, so she should have fed me some articulate, entertaining, and up-to-the-minute bragologue material to work with. Truth be told, the couple of times I had asked her to go into more detail about her professional background, she sloughed it off, saying, "Oh let's talk about something more interesting." Not a good sign! The meeting would have gone so much better had she taken the time beforehand to tell me—either verbally or in writing—exactly what she wanted me to say about herself and her services.

I can't stress enough the importance of making sure that people who are slated to introduce you or talk about you—at a luncheon, an industry panel, a keynote speech, or even a cocktail party—have their facts straight. We tend to believe we have little control over what others say, but more often than not people will simply repeat what they have heard from you. And if you haven't given them much material, they will try to drum something up, which is not very likely to hit the mark. Do your colleagues and friends have the right information about you? The difference can be dramatic, so make sure that you put the words you want them to use right into their mouths. Consider someone saying, "My friend Nina just went out on her own. She recently wrote the Web-site copy for a local auto repair shop" (true, but not very impressive), versus, "My friend Nina just converted her successful career in advertising into a freelance copywriting business. She's currently working on a promotional video for one of the largest retail chains in the U.S., among other assignments." A successful branding and bragging campaign is contingent upon getting the words right to begin with—and then making sure others use them when describing you.

KEEP YOUR VISIBILITY WHEN YOU'RE NOT FACE-TO-FACE.

It was a deal made in heaven.

Mark's employer, a publishing company, was moving its headquarters from its current location in Oregon to Colorado. Not wanting to unsettle his wife, who had a good job, and his children, who were doing well in school, Mark worked out a deal with the company whereby he could stay behind and work virtually from his home office.

Logistically, the arrangement had come off without a hitch. Projects were being completed on time and Mark's work hadn't suffered one iota from the distance. Things seemed to be humming along, until one day something happened that left him suddenly feeling insecure and even a bit hurt. Mark was left out of an impromptu meeting that the company's president had called concerning a major new competitor coming into the market. In the rush, no one had thought to bring Mark in by conference call. In fact, he didn't learn about the meeting until days later, and even then, only through a chance discussion with his boss. Next thing Mark knew, he was receiving e-mails that highlighted some of the decisions the group had made concerning how to respond to the threat. No one had even thought to ask for his opinion, which really upset him, given that he had a lot of knowledge about this particular competitor from dealing with them earlier in his career when working for another firm. Mark called me in a slight panic. Was this really just a case of oversight or was there something more sinister lurking here? Maybe he was reading way too much into it, but was this a sign that he was falling out of favor with his company? I told Mark that it was more likely a case of him falling off of management's radar, and that he had to get a plan in place fast to get back on it.

Telecommuting is one of the greatest inventions of the twenty-first century. But you have to make sure that you maintain a presence around the office or you will be out of sight and out of mind—and that you don't want! Often when people start to work virtually, they suddenly realize how much they had relied on informal and flyby networking for keeping colleagues and supervisors up to speed on their projects. When working together in a traditional office setting, people automatically come in contact with each other on a face-to-face basis. By working at home or in another town, you lose out on countless opportunities for connecting—everything from gathering around the proverbial watercooler to grabbing a bite to eat to chatting with someone in the ladies' room to even bumping into each other on weekends when your children play in the same sports league.

That's why it's imperative that when you go virtual, you put a "visibility" plan in place. In Mark's case, I asked him what he could do to remedy his situation, and he said that he had originally thought of paying a visit to headquarters, but then discounted it because "there was nothing big at the office coming up."

Classic virtual employee Mistake #1: Everyone thinks that there has to be some kind of major event for them to show up in person, initiate communication with people, or brag about themselves. Well, big things don't come around too often, so if you wait around for them, you might be waiting a long time.

Classic virtual employee Mistake #2: Mark thought he could correct the situation in one shot, but what he needed was an ongoing plan in place.

The good news is that by just becoming conscious of the need to stay visible when you're not face-to-face, you are halfway there. Once you recognize the need, you'll begin to see all sorts of opportunities, especially when you keep in mind the following suggestions for staying connected and on people's minds:

Target those people within your company who are important to helping you achieve your goals. Think of your career goals for the next three months and the next year, and ask yourself whose radar you need to be on to ensure success. This will not only include your boss, but your boss's boss, the president of the company, and influential people in other departments. Put together a short list of four to five people.

Determine how you are going to keep a constant thread to these people. This can be a combination of things, from scheduled in-person meetings with your boss to making sure you attend trade shows that many people from your company will be at to shooting someone on your list an e-mail saying, "I heard you were working on the XXX project. How's that going?" As previously mentioned, be sure to know the preferred method of communication for each of these four or five people. For example, does your boss like e-mail or voice mail? Once you've figured that out, at the end of each week, use the preferred communication vehicle to share a summary of what you've done. You can highlight your successes and the obstacles you've overcome, then describe what you're planning for the following week. That way, your boss knows what you have accomplished and what she can expect.

Don't underestimate the importance of face-to-face encounters. Nothing is quite as powerful as meeting face-to-face, even if it means flying to the East Coast from the West Coast just for that dreaded Christmas party. One woman, whose company was entirely virtual with no physical locations at all, made a point of taking some time to meet with her boss, who lived near to where she was vacationing with her family. When she was promoted six months later, she swore it was because she had made the effort to keep herself in front of her boss.

STOP CREDIT THIEVES IN THEIR TRACKS.

If I had a dime for every time someone came up to me and said, "I can't believe that I've been working on this project night and day for three weeks and my coworker just stole the credit," I would be a very rich woman.

Credit theft is endemic to the workplace. It happens constantly, often leaving people stunned and confused, especially in today's business environment, in which a premium is placed on the notion of "teamwork." Yet being a team player and being good at promoting yourself are *not* mutually exclusive. While teamwork is no doubt important, it shouldn't always be just about the team and not about your own contributions.

But what do you do if one of your teammates has particularly sharp elbows, steals your ideas, or is just an overall hog when it comes to claiming credit? First, before you get too huffy, take a deep breath and count to ten. If that doesn't calm you down, keep going in multiples of ten until you reach one hundred. After the first infraction, give your coworker the benefit of the doubt—assume that it wasn't malicious or malintended. If, however, you notice a pattern of similar behavior, take the person aside, calmly present the facts of the situation, and tell him that you would like him to stop. Keep your emotions out of it. Then cross your fingers that it doesn't continue. Of course, if it does, and you decide to do something further about it, then you'll need to step things up a bit and kick into what I call incremental escalation. This means you tell your colleague what the specific ramifications are going to be if he or she continues taking credit for your ideas and efforts.

For example, you spoke to Kyle in private after he took all the credit for a project you worked on together analyzing the financials for a particularly complex deal. Although he apologized, two weeks later he did it again. At that point, you could say to him, "Kyle, when we were in the meeting yesterday, you claimed sole responsibility for creating the agenda for the company's strategic-planning meeting. However, we both know that this is not the case and that I was very much a part of the work. In fact, I did most of it! Two weeks ago, when I pointed out your failure to acknowledge my role in working up those financials, you apologized and said it would not happen again. Well, it has, and now I'm telling you that next time, I'll let the others know then and there about my contributions. I don't want to embarrass you, Kyle, but this is not acceptable or appropriate. Credit needs to be given where it's due."

It's hard, it's scary, it's so unpleasant, but this is most likely what it will take to stop someone like Kyle.

The last suggestion for stopping credit thieves is to take a look at your own actions. Maybe people are taking the credit away from you simply because you've failed to take charge of your own self-promotion campaign, yet another good reason to put your brag campaign in place, as discussed earlier in this chapter.

Okay, I can hear it now: "But Peggy, what do I do if it's my boss—you know, the person who wields power in the relationship, who determines salaries, pay increases, bonuses, and whether I have a job in the first place?" This situation is always trickier. Bosses are being paid to manage people and to keep things moving. And nothing underscores successful management of a team more than a project that reaps results. So, on some level, bosses deserve the credit. When it comes to dealing with your boss, I would recommend that instead of counting to one hundred, you count to one thousand before doing anything. Stop and ask yourself, is this really about me or is it about my boss and, for whatever reason, the way she is or operates?

That's what Ron did, although it took every bone in his body to resist not going ballistic. There was his boss, Ruth, the group leader of the improvements committee, talking to a group of higher-ups about the tremendous response the committee's recent initiative had gotten for the company. She was coming off like the heroine of the day and, according to Ron, "conveniently not breathing a word of what happened behind the scenes to get those results." Ron had written the letter (which took days to get just right), updated the mailing list (which had been a complete mess), and sent everything out. To top it off, the entire project had an ungodly timetable. Ron had missed most of his son's base-ball season to meet the deadline.

I asked Ron a few questions.

Looking back at other meetings, had Ruth ever gone out of her way to compliment him or any of his teammates in public? No. In fact, when he really thought about it, he had never heard her compliment any of the team members in public.

Did Ruth ever recognize his efforts in other less-public ways? Mostly in performance reviews. Although on this project, she had said to him in passing, "Great job."

Had he consistently received increases in pay year to year? Yes.

So, all in all, it didn't seem that Ron was being unfairly targeted. In fact, it's not uncommon for managers to state up front that their policy is to never acknowledge individual contributions during presentations. Instead, acknowledgment will happen via the traditional methods of performance reviews, promotions, and/or pay increases. Perhaps this was the case with Ruth, who didn't want to appear to be playing favorites and thought it would undermine the team as a whole to single someone out.

Having thought about the various factors that Ron considered, if you still believe that your boss is not acting in good faith, then you have two options.

The first is to kick your bragging campaign into high gear so that others learn what you are up to, even if your boss isn't the one that tells them. There are plenty of opportunities for doing this, such as in hallway encounters, when standing in the cafeteria line, during the company barbeque, and at committee meetings. In the moment, you may be thinking that your boss is getting away with credit theft, but it won't matter much if you do your own bragging.

The second option is to approach your boss. Please notice that I used the word *approach,* not *confront*. Say something to this effect: "In your presentation last week, you didn't acknowledge my significant contribution on the project. Was there any particular reason why you chose not to?" Whatever you do, the last thing you want is to come across as accusatory or maligning his character.

As one person said to me, "Peggy, I'm shaking in my boots. I can't imagine saying anything to my boss. I'd just be too embarrassed and uncomfortable."

To which my response was "Stop shaking and start bragging."

Seven

HOT BUTTONS: GENDER, GENERATION, AND CULTURE

- Don't take it personally.

- Raise your sensitivity antenna.

- Competition is a double-edged sword.

- Find the silver lining.

- Stop stereotypes from sinking you.

The year was 1964. It was the Beatles' first appearance on *The Ed Sullivan Show* with 73 million people watching—a generational split-screen moment if there ever was one. During their second song, my father ejected himself from the sofa (a behavior he only exhibited when upset) and walked out of the den, shaking his head and muttering, "*This* is music?"

The world has continued to change and change and change since then. Nowadays, just as you might find a rich assortment of music—rock, classical, jazz, rap, hip-hop, pop, gospel, and the blues—happily coexisting on the same iPod, in most work environments you'll find tremendous diversity, from gender and age to ethnicity and culture. Yet without deft soft skills, the happily coexisting part doesn't come quite so easily.

Our workplace today is incredibly diverse and growing more so every minute as the forces of technology and globalization merge. The lessons in this chapter highlight the factors that cause us to see the world differently from each other and can bring about friction. Here you'll find a whole slew of soft skills for helping deal with issues of gender, generational, and cultural differences: emotional self-control, communication, empathy, motivating those who operate from a different competitive framework, finding the best in every person, and keeping ourselves in check when it comes to stereotyping.

DON'T TAKE IT PERSONALLY.

"I was humiliated."

"I felt so betrayed, and I'm not talking to him again until he apologizes."

While these quotes may sound like lines from the latest television soap opera, they are the actual words I often hear from women I coach. However, I've yet to find a man uttering these same phrases. I'm telling you about this somewhat curious gender difference to underscore the degree to which many women feel personally assaulted when someone criticizes them or their ideas. Research shows that, in general, women are the more empathetic sex and by nature more attuned to their own feelings and those of others. This is a good thing overall and a great advantage when dealing with human complexity. But there can be a downside to our emotional awareness—a huge downside: Woman often take things way too personally. And while being passionate is generally a positive thing, getting overly emotional on the job is a definite career sinker.

Once a woman gives into her tendency to overreact and reads too much into things when she's feeling challenged, disagreed with, or criticized on the job, there's trouble ahead. Matters get even worse if she lets herself succumb to what I call catastrophe creep: when she takes a piece of criticism and multiplies it by a thousand, then applies that criticism to her entire self instead of just the particular behavior, skill, or situation for which it was intended. Heightened feelings of insecurity and failure inevitably follow, which exacerbate the situation even more. While no doubt there are men who are also overly sensitive and take things too much to heart, they seem to be few and far between.

Cecilia's situation is a classic example of catastrophe creep. Her boss expressed disagreement regarding how to handle a particular problem with a client. He didn't even say, "I don't agree with you Cecilia." Rather, he asked for Cecilia's opinion, and then said, "I think the best way to go about it is this way . . ."—which wasn't anything near what Cecilia had proposed. No big deal. Case closed . . . you would think. But before she knew it, Cecilia went from "He didn't like my idea" to "Come to think of it, he didn't like that other idea I proposed three months ago" to "Come to *really* think of it, maybe I'm going to get fired!" By the time I met up with Cecilia, she was in a bad state. It took me two hours to unravel the events and trace it back to what her boss had offered as benign suggestion. Whereas a male colleague would likely take the boss's comment at face value and move on, Cecilia read far more into it than she should have, creating a subtext where none existed. In essence, she made a mountain out of a molehill. Instead of trying to understand what it was her boss didn't like about her proposal and countering him on the spot or figuring out how her reasoning was off base so she could do better the next time, Cecilia spent days ruminating and working herself into a highly unproductive frenzy. I'm exhausted just thinking back on it.

Crying on the job is one of the most extreme manifestations of emotional behavior at work. One male manager I coach was petrified in anticipation of the upcoming performance review of a female direct report. During her previous two reviews, she had broken down crying at the slightest criticism, causing him to end the meetings before he had the chance to make all of his points. By holding him an emotional hostage—whether intentionally or not—the employee was able to get exactly what she wanted, which in this case was to avoid criticism. I pointed out to him how unproductive this outcome was for both of them and advised him to write down what was making him so uncomfortable about her reactions. Then—to shore up his confidence for the upcoming session—I instructed him to write out the reasons why, as her boss, he needed to finish the review even if she played the crying card again. I suggested that if she broke down, he should respond with empathy, saying, "I can see that you are becoming upset," while at the same time offering the woman some Kleenex and asking her to take fifteen minutes to collect herself, then come back to his office to resume the meeting. If she continued to cry upon returning, he should hand her some more Kleenex, tell her to take a moment, then continue. He could also offer some specific behaviors that she could do to manage her emotions, but should in no way let her tears run the meeting.

Displaying waterworks on the job sets women back. In fact, when I did it once in my mid-twenties and told my sister Nancy about it, she said, "Peggy, you've just set feminism back twenty years." I didn't think it was as dire as all that, but I knew from then on I would try never to do it again. Crying on the job often derails discussions, causing coworkers and managers to feel very uncomfortable. Worse yet, the sob factor can make colleagues see you as not being tough enough to succeed in the business world and prompt them to perceive your crying as manipulation to get what you want. One friend of mine, Connie, who runs an entertainment company, recalled years ago pulling aside a junior staff member who cried in a client meeting and telling her, "If you ever do that again in a business situation, you're fired." She never did, and today she's Connie's business partner.

If you feel like your emotions are about to get the best of you, keep the following in mind:

- Short of the rare occurrence of receiving unexpected personal news of a serious nature or when shedding tears of joy, don't weep at work. If you become upset about something job-related and you simply can't help yourself, quickly head for the privacy of a bathroom stall. It may not be the most comfortable place, but you can shut the door and stay there until you've gotten it out of your system and composed yourself.

- Learn to separate your personal identity from the deal, project, or discussion at hand. When someone questions your opinion or judgment, don't take it as rejection. Remind yourself that differing viewpoints often lead to more creative solutions for getting the job done. Never equate being challenged at work with someone saying, "I don't like you." Instead, remind yourself that disagreement is a natural part of doing business.

- Preparation is the best defense. People trip up when they don't prepare ahead of time for situations that they know are going to be difficult. You'll be better able to ward off overreacting in the event the discussions heats up if you confront your emotional hot buttons in advance. Prepare by asking yourself the "what ifs," as in "What if he wants to talk about that report again?" or "What if Patricia challenges me about my approach to the project?"

- Watch your body language and vocal tone when you feel yourself getting emotional. Whereas men tend to become louder and more expansive when upset, using their bodies to take up space and gesticulate broadly, women tend to physically contract, almost collapsing into themselves and appearing smaller in stature. Like an orangutan, their shoulders slump forward and their bodies become concave, as if they want to disappear. Their voices often lose volume and become either very high-pitched and squeaky, like an adolescent, or very soft and breathy, like a seductress.

- Some women I've coached react to stressful situations by suddenly turning red from the chest up through the neck. I don't know the medical reason for this flushing phenomenon, but deep breathing and other relaxation techniques can sometimes prevent it from occurring. If you suffer from this physical response to stress, consider wearing a scarf or a turtleneck on the days you anticipate a particularly difficult meeting, conversation, or interaction.

- If all else fails and you feel yourself slipping, take deep breaths. The oxygen will help clear your mind and calm you down.

RAISE YOUR SENSITIVITY ANTENNA.

Okay, guys, not so fast there. Just because I tell people not to cry on the job doesn't mean we stop being human beings once we get to the office. Staying tuned in to emotions is definitely an important workplace soft skill that everyone needs to possess, particularly those in managerial or leadership roles. Unfortunately, though, just as some women can be overly sensitive, some men are known for being too insensitive. That's hardly surprising news. And while it's true that we've been undergoing tremendous cultural shifts in these areas, most parents still aren't giving their boys dolls to play with while they are growing up.

If you're a guy reading this, I can envision you right now rolling your eyes. But before you go there, I want you to know that I am not talking about being more sensitive for sensitivity's sake or proposing that you embrace a warm-and-fuzzy approach. Take a minute to recognize how reaching out and acknowledging what others around you are feeling can have a dramatic effect on job satisfaction and performance. Let me show you a very simple example of how a small gesture, in this case just a twist of words, can make all the difference.

Sam walked into his bimonthly staff meeting with the fourteen people in his department and immediately got down to business saying, "Okay, everyone. We've got a lot of work to do today and not a lot of time, so let's get going!" Under normal circumstances, his staff might have let him get away with such a cursory opening. But on that particular day, he was completely ignoring that one staff member had just returned from maternity leave and that it was the first day back for another who had taken some time off after his father suddenly passed away. Sam thought that if he took a minute to acknowledge any of this, the meeting would turn into some kind of therapy session, diverting time and attention away from the urgent business at hand.

Privately, what did Sam's staff say about him after the meeting?

"What a jerk. How could he not congratulate Donna on the baby or express his condolences to Roger? Doesn't he care?"

It would have taken Sam less than a minute to welcome Donna back from maternity leave and say, "I was sorry to hear about your father, Roger. I've been thinking about you." But Sam was like many other men. In his book, there was no room for what he considered small talk—which he defined as "inconsequential and distracting chatter unrelated to business." What he didn't recognize is that small talk is a crucial part of making connections with others. It's about putting everyone at ease and creating a comfortable environment, much like you would for your dinner guests. It's also about treating people like people, rather than treating them like drones. Improving the workplace environment, and ultimately the bottom line, is about being sincere and creating an authentic link with others—be they your customers, colleagues, bosses, employees, or even total strangers.

COMPETITION IS A DOUBLE-EDGED SWORD.

"Peggy, he practically slammed the Ping-Pong ball practically down my throat! What's his problem? Does he have to win at everything—even during a friendly game at the corporate picnic?"

Say no more. Men and women are on separate wavelengths when it comes to competition, and understanding those differences can bring us a long way toward making each gender more effective at work.

Although men generally love competition and breathe it like air, women as a group don't seem to enjoy it as much. Recent research found that women participants were twice as likely to select a noncompetitive setting over a tournament-style one when given the choice—even when they are equally competent at performing a particular task. Even now, as young girls are increasingly engaging in team sports, it remains to be seen whether their attitudes toward competition will change. For the time being, however, one thing seems for sure: if women want to get ahead in the corporate world, they need to "suit up" into a more competitive frame of mind.

Fifty-one-year-old Celine represents what I believe is happening with a lot of women, particularly baby boomers. After months of soul-searching about her job, she had come to me for advice on how to take her career to the next level. Well respected by her colleagues, Celine was moving up the ladder, but at a slower pace than she wanted. When we dove into the details of what was holding her back to date, Celine blamed it on a number of outside factors beyond her control. And yet, in every instance, some other man or woman with the same level of skill and experience had eventually been promoted over her.

When I asked Celine to describe her competition for the promotion she was currently going for, here is what she said:

"Her name is Kathy. She's really a nice person and she's worked very hard, too."

Celine didn't have to say another word. My hunch, which proved to be right, was that her views on competition were holding her back. For many women, competition often carries a "you're not nice" subtext or suggests that, as Celine put it bluntly, "You're a bitch; you're aggressive; you only care about yourself." Celine had been raised to be a promoter, nurturer, and cheerleader for others rather than to focus on her own goals and talents. Her feelings on competition had put her in a double bind. On one hand, she had the talent and the drive to succeed, but on the other hand, she felt uncomfortable with the notion of pitting herself against someone else, especially a friend whom she saw as being so nice and equally qualified. She didn't want the responsibility or the guilt of beating Kathy out for the promotion, and she certainly didn't want to destroy their relationship. Celine was, ironically, more afraid of winning than of losing.

To get Celine on track, she first had to recognize that her beliefs about competing were holding her back. As much as she didn't like the zero-sum game, the fact was that only one person was going to land this particular job and title at this particular time. So she had to decide if she wanted it enough to change her behavior—even though doing so would be uncomfortable and painful at times. Once we got over that hurdle, Celine outlined her goals so we could construct short-term and long-term career plans, which included a detailed strategy for winning the promotion that had sparked the entire process in the first place.

And what about the guy at the beginning of this section who had to beat everyone at Ping-Pong at his corporate picnic? What would be useful for him and others like him to know?

First, if you want to get the best out of your female employees and teammates, or have clients who are female, be extra aware of your competitive streak. Since men as a rule are more motivated by competition than women, they have the tendency to turn even noncompetitive situations into competitive ones. If you have this tendency and are unaware of it, you'll likely come across as less than gracious or, even worse yet, obnoxious. While other men will likely understand and not take offense at your overzealous competing, when working across the gender lines, this behavior is usually offensive.

Equally important, if you are in a management position and have a mostly female team, you will get more out of them if you create an environment that acknowledges what best motivates them. For example, consider using a collaborative approach when setting up an incentive program so that everyone on the team can benefit from hard work, rather than using a winner-takes-all reward system.

FIND THE SILVER LINING.

Sherry, the forty-nine-year-old founder of a retail business, was frustrated with her administrative assistant, Amber, a woman in her early twenties. Amber was chronically late to work. And even when she arrived on time, she would often leave earlier than she should. Sherry had let her get away with it a few times, but now it was getting out of hand, and it was long past time to put her foot down.

"Peggy, I don't get it. Amber's good at her work when she gets here. She says this is the field she wants to be in, but she acts like her career is a low priority. I'm beginning to think she doesn't care enough about the job and that I might need to fire her."

What Sherry didn't understand is that Amber, like many others of her generation, had grown up seeing her mom—the director of client services for an employment firm—put in very long hours at her job. Amber made the decision early on that she didn't want that kind of stress and that she wanted a life that was more than just her career. Her values were decidedly different from those of Sherry and her mom, who thought nothing of working sixty-hour weeks. Amber didn't want to sacrifice her personal life for her career like they had. No way, no how.

When we think of diversity in the workplace, race and gender often come to mind. But there's another dimension causing major tensions these days. Age. For the first time, four generations of workers are coexisting at once: the matures (born before 1945), the baby boomers (born between 1946 and 1964), the Gen Xers (born between 1965 and 1980), and the Millennials—also known as Generation Y (born after 1980).

It's not always a pretty scene when the older and younger generations collide in the workplace. "Who do they think they are?" is the comment I often hear from older workers griping about their younger counterparts. "They think they should have my job at twenty-six, yet they aren't willing to put in the time. They may have the book smarts and their fancy MBAs, but they don't have the real-life experience. I can tell you that life looks a lot different from outside the classroom."

As an older banker wondered, "What is it with their short attention spans? Do they always need to be on their BlackBerrys or cell phones? I'll be leading a meeting and look up to see everyone under thirty text messaging. You never have one hundred percent of their attention. They seem to need constant interaction and connection with their buddies. Older people are far more independent. We don't always need to be doing everything with someone else."

Sometimes I hear women in their thirties and forties complain that they've encountered the most resistance and competition not from men, but from female bosses who are baby boomers or older and think, "Hey, I'm not going to help them; no one helped me." Or "If I lend them a hand, they might take what I have."

Having fought so hard to make inroads in the male-dominated work world, older women sometimes suffer from a scarcity mentality, meaning that they see so few jobs at the top available to them that they want to keep competition to a minimum. The net result: they are less likely to engage in mentoring relationships with Gen Xers. Even if Generation Yers pose less of a threat, lending them a helping hand isn't a concept successful older women take to so easily. As one seasoned manager commented, "Why should I help someone who doesn't invest in her career? I worked long and hard hours, while many of my younger staffers tend to be nine-to-fivers.

Conversely, and not surprisingly, how the younger generations view their elders at work isn't any prettier. These are some of the things I hear them say about the older generations:

- "They are so stuck in the past and rigid about the way things should be done."

- "They don't want to change anything."

- "We are never going to get anywhere in the company because they aren't going to retire when they should. They're hanging on forever."

- "In order to get things done, we really need to get them out."

I hate to be the mother hen here, but this situation isn't going to improve until both the younger and the older generations learn to live with each other—and the sooner the better. The reality is that younger people are increasingly given titles and salaries way ahead of their time, a trend that is unlikely to reverse itself. The days of working in the stockroom for a couple of years and being groomed over time—so you actually knew what you were doing before you were promoted to a certain level—are fast fading. Now people are thrown in and pretty much expected to sink or swim. On top of that, the baby boomers aren't going away any time soon. Many can't afford to retire, and, even if they could, research suggests that they plan to stick around as long as possible because they find their careers both stimulating and fulfilling.

If you are looking to navigate generational differences, the most important thing you can do is simply this: be respectful. No matter what generation you are from, recognize that every single person has something to offer. As I often say, "I don't care if it's the person who sweeps the streets or it's the chairman of the company, when you find yourself feeling challenged by differences, ask yourself: What can this person teach me?" When you work from a sense of openness and curiosity, you'll most likely "find the silver lining," as one of my clients put it.

That's what Sheila found.

A forty-eight-year-old sales director, Sheila was often pitching to the younger buyers in her region. In a call to a potential buyer, one of her twentysomething sales associates overheard her saying, "Let's hook up sometime next week." The associate took Sheila aside and advised, "When you use the expression 'hooking up' with people my age, it means getting together in a sexual way. I'm sure it doesn't suggest that to you and you didn't intend it that way, but you should know about this when dealing with the younger buyers." Sheila was so thankful for this younger woman's advice about her generational faux pas that she asked her to put together a list of words and phrases—what she now calls her Gen X/Y dictionary—so she can speak their language better.

Sixtysomething George found the silver lining, too.

One of the most senior publishing executives in the office, George held a pretty negative view of younger employees, at least until the day he needed a digital photo fixed fast. It was late in the evening when he popped his head out of his office to see if anyone was still around. The only person left was Eric, a twenty-three-year-old editorial assistant who was staying late to finish a report due the next morning. George asked Eric if he knew how to use "that Photoshop stuff" and if he might be able to fix something for him that he needed to send off that night. Eric scanned the image and quickly cleaned it up. As George later conveyed to me, "Eric wasn't even from the graphics department, but that didn't seem to matter. He knew his way around the software and was glad to help. It would have taken me hours to figure out how to do what he did to that photo in ten minutes." From that point on, the two developed a comfortable working relationship, and George eventually invited the younger man to be part of a brainstorming team on a new project. Said George, "Once I took the blinders off and got past my prejudices, I started to appreciate more what the newer hires are bringing to the table. Before Eric helped me out that night, I thought of him as another too-loud and cocky twentysomething. But now I've come to appreciate the energy and curiosity he brings. Eric asks questions my older colleagues won't go near—their experience has turned them into a bunch of naysayers! He's still open to the possibilities, which I find refreshing."

Perhaps one of my favorite cross-generation stories is this.

One aspiring thirtysomething female leader at a Wall Street investment house went to bat for an older gentleman in his late fifties during her firm's bonus and promotion season. The firm was handing out the coveted title of managing director and, along with it, its many perks. Recalling the situation, she said, "Peggy, I went before a group of senior executives and made a pitch for Leon to make managing director. He had been with the firm for nearly twenty years, but really contributed to building our business when we opened a new office three years ago. Even though I'm a good twenty-five years his junior and his boss, I very much appreciated knowing that he had that region covered, and covered well. It took a tremendous load off my mind during my first years in management and allowed me to focus on other areas in far greater need. For some reason, Leon got overlooked years ago when it came to handing out managing director titles." When she presented the idea to her higher-ups, they were less than enthused. Didn't she know that if he hadn't made managing director by now, it was too late? But his young advocate was unfazed. She continued over the course of a couple meetings to try to convince them otherwise, and, in the end, succeeded. As she remembered, "When I called Leon to tell him about his new title, he practically fell off his chair. Although he certainly never said it, believe me, I knew that the last thing he thought when I came on was that I would take the time to do something like this for him."

STOP STEREOTYPES FROM SINKING YOU.

Recently, I gave a leadership seminar to a group of professionals based in Switzerland for a major Fortune 500 company. It was a mixed-gender group of senior executives.

I was forewarned by various people that I should be prepared for a rather stiff, formal reception and that I might want to consider taking my enthusiastic style down a notch (translation: do away with the clapping and whistles). Some colleagues who had recently worked in Switzerland shared with me that the Swiss nature was more conservative than I was used to and it would take a lot of work to get them to talk about themselves. In other words, I should be prepared to drag things out of them.

To my delight, nothing could have been farther from the truth.

My Swiss executives were exceedingly open and talkative about their own professional development challenges, and were immediately able to adjust to my brand of experiential learning. How could my advisers have gotten it so wrong?

Stereotypes!

Right or wrong, we still tend to categorize people who are different from ourselves. Doing so today is proving increasingly risky with globalization upon us, blurring the cultural lines within the business world.

Take my friend Aiko, whose mother is Japanese and father is Korean. Aiko moved to England from Japan when she was six, then to the United States at the age of nine. As an adult, she has returned to Asia to work; there, she is seen as being far too brash. But even her American associates think she is too outspoken, and, truthfully, if I were her coach, I would actually tell her to "tone it down" a bit. So much for the quiet and subservient Asian-woman stereotype. One of my clients is part Filipino and part German. Another is part Argentinean, part Canadian. And another could hold United Nations events at his family reunions. What category do these people fit in?

For all their good intentions, even diversity programs can sometimes limit us and feed into stereotyping by overfocusing on placing people into categories, which can work against us, even when we are dealing with someone in our own category. For instance, we might think we are very similar to someone who is the same religion or ethnicity, when in fact we have nothing in common with that person at all. Just as likely, we can be misled into thinking we are very different than someone from another group, when in fact we are surprisingly alike.

Last year, I met a woman from Wyoming who appeared at first glance to have an uncanny likeness to me. We were speakers at the same women's leadership conference and are both short, Caucasian, professional women of about the same age, with similar coloring and haircuts. Later, when we sat next to each other at lunch, I realized that we were far less similar than anyone would have expected. Indeed, I quickly realized I have much more in common with the male client I had met with the previous week—a six-foot-tall sports agent who was born in India and now lived in New York. My Wyoming colleague was raised on a ranch, still lives in the country, and adores country music, whereas the trader and I share a love of urban life and the opera.

A close colleague of mine was transferred from Manhattan to Rome years ago. She had expected that her biggest challenge would be learning to work at a slower pace with the southern Italians. But what she found instead was that the Italians were the easiest part of her adjustment. "What was hardest culturally was dealing with my boss, who was British. Given our common language, not to mention the strong history between Great Britain and the United States, I thought that we would have the same sensibilities and get along fine—or famously, as he would have put it. But instead, we knocked heads constantly and had entirely different approaches to just about everything—not to mention his not-so-hidden dislike of Americans!"

Speaking of disliking Americans, it's humbling to take a look at some of the stereotypes people from other countries have about the United States. For example, a group of high school and college students from Spain—who have never been to the United States—compiled the following list: Americans are mostly very tall and have blue eyes with blond hair. The women are either very fat or very thin, never average, and they all wear a ton of makeup. Most of their time is spent working, although they say that family comes first. Movies and rodeos are their favorite leisure pastimes. Their homes are either in skyscrapers or on farms and they all drive Cadillacs—unless they live on the farms, in which case they travel by horseback. Due to their very dangerous cities, American men all carry guns. Their diet consists of almost nothing but junk food and they eat humongous breakfasts. Coke and beer are their drinks of choice. When they speak, they are quick and loud, not to mention rude. And when it comes to everything from international affairs to their personal lives, they do whatever the heck they want and couldn't care less what other people think.

If you are an American, does what you just read sound like you and everyone you know? Probably not! At its best, stereotyping is a way of processing vast amounts of data in an attempt to make sense of people who seem unfamiliar. At its worst, it lulls us into thinking we already understand them so we don't have to bother getting to know them for real. Stereotypes also reinforce the superiority of our own ways of thinking and doing things. As human beings, we will probably never entirely stop categorizing each other, but we can acknowledge the limitations of stereotyping and learn to catch ourselves doing it. As you deal with people who are different from you, keep the following in mind:

- First, know thyself. Look at and understand your biases, your preferences, and what buttons are pushed when you are dealing with people who are different from you.

- Accept that differences are inherent rather than a hassle, an inconvenience to be gotten over, or a problem to be solved.

- Focus on the qualities of each individual, rather than the stereotypes about the categories they may fit into.

- Avoid making assumptions. If you don't understand why someone is doing something, ask questions.

- Don't tolerate insensitive behavior toward you or anyone else.

Eight

LEADING THE TROOPS

- Know what you're getting into.

- A good manager knows when to lead.

- Avoid being a know-it-all, say-it-all, control-it-all kind of boss.

- People aren't mind readers.

- You're the boss, stupid, that's why they hang on your every word.

- Treat everyone equally.

- The impostor syndrome will follow you up the ladder.

- A little humility takes you a long way.

At the beginning of my career, I thought that managers were those people with big titles who oversaw lots of other workers. But I soon came to realize that—even though my job title didn't reflect it—I had become a manager the day I was assigned my first production assistant and became responsible for giving him things to do. The trick, it turned out, was making sure he got them done in the best way possible, which I quickly found was easier said than done.

For many, the holy grail of their career is a position in management. Others, however, think supervising someone else should be avoided at any cost. In the end, workers from both camps are promoted to supervisory positions. And when they are—whether pursuer or avoider—they frequently start out with a dangerous lack of expertise in the soft skill of leadership and what it takes to successfully rally the troops. Unfortunately, management training programs within companies—when they exist at all—are often cursory or even subscribe to the mistaken assumption that a strong set of technical competencies and longevity on the job are the best preparation.

In this final chapter, we'll highlight some of the most important soft skills just beneath the surface of good leadership, including knowing your strengths and weaknesses, taking the initiative to address your shortcomings, influencing and motivating people to think and act the way you want, letting others express their ideas and trusting them to do the job, expressing your needs and goals clearly, being mindful of all your communication, treating everyone with respect regardless of rank, and last but not least—drum roll, please—swallowing a good serving of humble pie every so often.

KNOW WHAT YOU'RE GETTING INTO.

There seems to be no shortage of bad bosses in the workplace. Recent movies and tell-all books have immortalized them. The problem has become so widespread that there are entire training programs (including some of my own) solely dedicated to dealing with the various types of difficult supervisors. If you become a manager, the last thing you want is to find yourself on the following list of bad-boss types.

Exploders possess a horrific and unpredictable temper. It's never clear what's going to set them off. Imagine working for Dr.

Jekyll and Mr. Hyde or with a ticking time bomb that could go off at any minute.

Charmers are just that—charmingly agreeable, affable, delightful to be around, and people you think you can confide in. But watch out. Later they will stab you in the back, pit you against another employee, reveal secrets and ideas that you've told them, or whittle away at your authority behind the scenes.

Wet blankets earn their name by dampening everything around them and shooting down ideas with lines such as "We've been there, done that, and I know it won't work." Their motto? No can do.

Know-it-alls hate to appear vulnerable or to seem like they don't know what they are doing and will protect their top-dog status at any cost. They don't ask for anyone else's opinion and are convinced that their own ideas are always the best.

So why are bad bosses running rampant these days?

The explanation is simple. A bad boss is born each time someone goes into management without knowing what he is really getting into or receiving the training he needs to be effective. When initially offered the job, instead of asking whether they are suited or equipped for the tasks and the stress of being a manager, people quickly become intoxicated by the thought of more power and a bigger salary. Maybe they're attracted to the notion of fame and fortune associated with those incredibly mythic leaders from history like George Washington and Thomas Jefferson or the more contemporary titans of industry like Bill Gates, Meg Whitman, and Jack Welch. Or they worry that refusing the job will stall their career. They rarely stop to think about the enormous time commitment and learning curve ahead as they transition from being a successful individual contributor to managing a group of diverse people. They often fail to consider the demands of an expanding work schedule, hiring/training/supervising/firing staff, developing a vision and tactical strategy, creating budgets, being accountable for the productivity of others, and so on.

Simon, a star salesperson on Wall Street, had a serious case of sticker shock after finally being promoted to managing director. Similar to not knowing how expensive a car was really going to be by the time you added in taxes, insurance, and maintenance, he was unprepared for the realities of overseeing a group of seasoned traders who had been his colleagues for seven years. Simon jumped into the fire without a mentor or a single management-training course, and, within a year, it was mutiny on the sales desk. His team quickly turned into a school of barracudas and devoured his authority. By the time Simon called me for help, he was essentially powerless and wondered if there was any hope for the situation. As we talked, it became clear that although it was probably too late to turn around his group, what he really wanted was to turn back the clock. On the strength of his performance prior to taking on the new position, and after lengthy negotiations to restructure his job description, Simon was able to return to his former role of individual contributor while still retaining the managing director title. At last report, he's now a much happier fellow.

The lesson? When offered a management position, don't take the leap without first finding out the *real* scoop on what you'll be getting into. Talk to your future boss, the person you would be replacing, team members, and anyone else who can help fill you in on what the job will actually entail. One of the best ways to avoid sticker shock, however, is to take an honest look at your own strengths, limitations, and motivations before saying yes. Start by asking yourself these questions:

Do you . . .

. . . enjoy working with people, helping them grow and be successful?

. . . handle uncertainty well?

. . . mind making decisions without knowing the entire picture?

. . . need everyone to like you?

. . . want immediate and constant reinforcement?

. . . feel nervous about having legal and financial responsibilities for others?

. . . communicate well, in good times and bad?

. . . balk at the idea of evaluating or firing someone?

. . . have the time in your life to take this on?

People often ask me whether being a successful manager is a learned skill or, like athletic prowess or a great singing voice, something you're simply born with. The short answer is that even tremendously talented NBA players and opera divas must hone their innate abilities with a lot of practice—and the same holds true for excelling at management. Although some people seem to come by it naturally and others prove never to be good at it at all, the vast majority achieves excellence though a combination of learning the right skills and hard work.

Last, it's absolutely imperative that you find out what kind of leadership training the company offers before taking the leap, especially if you are new to management. Ask yourself how your company is going to help you succeed. Does it routinely provide training at this level and for this job? How about mentoring support on an ongoing basis? Often people don't even think to find out what's available. Even fairly senior executives who should have asked for resources up front, don't. As one executive said, exasperated after his first attempt at leading a department was a complete debacle, "It's hard to ask for help because everyone is applauding you by offering you the job. If you ask for help at the start, they might not think you are ready." Better to risk them thinking that than to charge ahead without the support you need to succeed!

Remember that you don't have to say yes. Depending on the field and company you are working in, there are other ways besides management to further your career. One thing is for certain: the more you are perceived as being really good at what you do, the more able you'll be to carve out the path you want—whether in management or not.

A GOOD MANAGER KNOWS WHEN TO LEAD.

Academia often debates the difference between leaders and managers. A leader is the person at the top, responsible for the strategy, the big picture, the view from thirty thousand feet away. A manager, on the other hand, is the one on the ground level who is more tactical and takes care of the day-to-day operations of the business and troops.

In real life versus textbooks, good managers constantly call on their leadership skills, and people in leadership positions wrestle with management issues. So regardless of your official job description, you have to be skilled at both.

For example, if you are a leader and you want your brilliant strategy to be implemented, you better be able to sell it to management. Once that's done, then you need to make sure that your vision is being executed properly. Conversely, as a manager, you will be called upon to cope with change, set direction, motivate your team, challenge people when they aren't delivering, and all the other leadership-like qualities that affect outcome. Companies nowadays expect managers to exhibit strong leadership skills. Otherwise, employees will be running for the competition.

Take Larry's firm. It had recently undergone a major downsizing. As a senior manager, Larry not only had to let people go, which was bad enough, but he also had to deal with those who were still left—many of whom were shell-shocked that their friends and colleagues were gone, angry that they now had more work than ever before without a corresponding increase in salary, and worried about being next on the chopping block. Larry knew that to help his group "get back in the game," he was going to have to step up to the plate with his leadership skills to set a positive tone, motivate the disgruntled team, and implement new programs that reflected the company's current reality. Gathering everyone for a meeting, he was up front with his group and constructively framed what was happening, saying, "No doubt we have been through some rough times and there are more ahead, but the firm is ultimately trying to make things better. I want you all to be here with me when that happens, so we need to work through this together to get there." Larry also let his team know that he believed in them and would be right there with them every step of the way. At the end of the meeting, he also introduced a new bonus system linked to mission-critical activities. He had spent weeks selling this incentive program to the higher-ups because, as Larry explained to me, "telling my team to just buck up wasn't going to fly."

Now imagine for a second if Larry had been stuck in the textbook definition of a manager as the day-to-day, nose-to-the-grindstone taskmaster who focuses on execution only. Managers who also know how to lead make all the difference when a company changes shape—whether from downsizing, merging, or adjusting to new marketplace challenges.

There's simply no debating it.

AVOID BEING A KNOW-IT-ALL, SAY-IT-ALL, CONTROL-IT-ALL KIND OF BOSS.

Once we become a manager, there's a strong tendency to think we are supposed to know everything. But as soon as we start down the know-it-all path, say-it-all and control-it-all behaviors quickly follow. You might be thinking, "Well, what's so wrong with that? After all, new managers got where they are by really knowing their business, right? After years of listening and being told what to do by others, isn't it now their turn to do the talking? And, since the buck stops right at their desk, isn't it their job to keep everything under control?"

While this might seem like sound reasoning, it's not. In practice, this argument is a recipe for disaster. If you don't allow your employees to bring their thoughts and ideas to the table, if you never *really* listen to them, and if you micromanage every moment of their workday, then resentment is just around the corner and productivity will drop. And if that didn't convince you, maybe this will: being a know-it-all boss will undo you sooner or later, as Derrick and countless others have found.

Derrick was micromanaging his project team so intensely that his promotion to partner was in jeopardy. He had been told that his inability to delegate was putting his leadership skills in question. Case in point: Derrick had been staying up night after night, reworking the PowerPoint his team was putting together for an upcoming presentation. Although he kept sending it back to them for additional research and other improvements, the changes were never done to his satisfaction. In our sessions to-

gether, we worked on learning how to give his team the information, tools, and resources up front that they need to get the job
done right without his constant interventions. For the presentation materials, that meant being specific about every detail—from
writing style to graphics and organization of the slides, even
down to the preferred font. Once he started making his expectations clear from the get-go, his team was able to move forward on
its own. Derrick could then review the work and send it back
with detailed instructions for further modification, if needed. He
was able to get a good night's sleep again, and his firm's fear that
he couldn't "get out of the weeds" with his team evaporated. Derrick now calls himself a quality freak, replacing the previous
behind-his-back moniker of control freak.

The feeling of needing to know it all is one of the hardest
things for managers to overcome. Another client confessed how
embarrassed he felt at a recent meeting. In front of a colleague
from his senior management team and the company's president,
he had to admit that he wasn't up to speed on something that he
probably should have understood better. But the truth is that the
learning process never ends. No one can know it all, even the
CEO. Part of becoming a great manager is to model for your
team how to find out what you don't know, rather than hiding it.

Another manager had become obsessed about coming to meetings with the answers to everything. Her breakthrough moment
was the realization that she didn't need to be perfect to be effective. "When I first became a manager, I wanted to earn people's
respect by showcasing my technical knowledge and skills—after
all, they had made me successful as an individual performer. It finally dawned on me that my new job was about facilitating the
meetings, not dominating them. I became a good manager by
drawing out what everyone else has to offer."

PEOPLE AREN'T MIND READERS.

"Peggy, I can't take it anymore," said Phoebe, the head of HR for a major health care company, adding, "I am having so many issues with people on my team, but they just don't seem to be getting it."

"Getting what?" I asked.

"Well, Josh needs to be more of a team player. Sophie's time management is a disaster. And Robin should be a better statesman. It feels like a ten-car pileup on the highway."

"Tell me more," I said, "and be specific."

Phoebe responded by continuing on, practically repeating word for word what she had said to me only a nanosecond earlier.

She didn't have to say another thing. I already understood why her team members were not "getting it."

Although Phoebe thought she was being very clear, she wasn't being specific at all.

In every workplace situation, especially when you're leading the troops, precision in your communication makes a dramatic difference. Unfortunately, much of what managers say is vague and amorphous. Their input is way too general and opens the door for multiple interpretations, most of them wrong. When giving feedback, for instance, people can only meet your requests or change their behavior if they are specifically told what they need to do differently. In the case of Josh, Phoebe never gave him specific examples that pointed out when he wasn't acting like a team player and what specifically it would take to become one at the company. In the case of Sophie, Phoebe never offered her clear suggestions for improving her time-management skills, such as to prioritize tasks, set deadlines, prevent interruptions when under deadline, and delegate more administrative tasks to the assistant.

And when it came to Phoebe's comment that Robin needed to be a better statesman, I had completely misunderstood what Phoebe was getting at. I had imagined that she meant Robin should project more confidence, and perhaps lower the pitch of her voice. But that wasn't at all what Phoebe had in mind. No wonder Robin wasn't making the expected changes—she probably had no idea what they were.

What Phoebe really meant was that Robin had been turning off a lot of the higher-ups because of her undiplomatic reactions to their suggestions and ideas in meetings. Instead of answering with the brusque response "It won't work," she needed to ask them in a friendly tone how they had arrived at their opinions. Then Robin should explain that she and her team had considered that idea already and had ultimately abandoned it because of x, y, and z reasons. This is the kind of specific advice that Phoebe needed to be giving Robin.

Unfortunately, when it comes to managing people, the lack of specificity isn't limited to giving employees feedback. Often when assigning projects, managers leave out the all-important why, when, and how. They don't explain the context of why the project is needed and critical; they don't provide a timeline for completion; and they don't specify how they want the person or group to approach the assignment.

While there will never be a magic wand for improving workplace communication, once managers learn to be specific, they might just think they have found one. Here are a few tips to get you started:

- Write "be specific" on a Post-it and stick it on your office wall. Write the same two words on the notes you take into meetings with you. Each time you look at the Post-it or down at your notes, you will be reminded to be specific.

- Illustrate your points by giving clear examples of actual situations.

- Refer to specific behaviors when giving feedback.

- Paint a detailed picture of the scenarios you are talking about.

- Describe how you want things to be handled differently in the future—for example, "Next time, I would like you to tell me your concerns about my performance in private rather than in front of the group."

- Avoid diluting your message with qualifying statements such as "sort of" or "kind of."

YOU'RE THE BOSS, STUPID, THAT'S WHY THEY HANG ON YOUR EVERY WORD.

What you say takes on a whole new significance once you become the boss. You now hold sway over people's livelihoods—everything from whether they get to the next level to their raises and bonuses. Every statement you make, and even your nonverbal gestures, will be put under the microscope for signs of hidden meaning and motive. Unfortunately, the net result is that others can greatly magnify or misconstrue your words.

Take, for example, the boss who told his colleagues during some casual Monday morning banter that he had come in to the office over the weekend. "At the time I said it, I didn't think anything of it, Peggy, although looking back, I have to admit it was met with a dead silence," said Raymond during one of our coaching sessions.

Turns out that while some of Raymond's reports hardly gave his comment a second thought, a couple of the "nose-to-the-grindstone" types did. As the week came to a close, Raymond dropped in on one of them, Amanda, on his way out of the office. She mentioned her plans to come in to work over the weekend. When Raymond asked why, she replied that she thought he might want her help on the major restructuring project, something they had been working on for months.

There was only one small problem with Amanda's offer: Raymond had absolutely no intention of working that weekend. Indeed, he was taken aback that Amanda assumed he would be there at all. Suddenly, Raymond realized that she must have read the wrong meaning into his passing comments earlier in the week. While he appreciated her dedication and work ethic, Amanda was missing a critical piece of information about why Raymond had been in the office the Sunday before. Turns out that he had left some insurance forms on his desk that needed to be filled out and turned in first thing Monday morning, otherwise his health benefits would lapse. His being there the previous weekend had nothing at all to do with working on the project.

The way you communicate peer-to-peer often won't fly when you communicate supervisor-to-staff. Much as with a parent talking to a child, your words have amplified power and you need to be far more mindful about what you say. Unless you've worked with your staff for an extended period, which is less and less likely these days, you no longer have the freedom to "freethink"—that is, babble away and say things off the top of your head. We've all heard stories of people scrambling about and working on various new initiatives, only to realize—sometimes days, if not weeks later—that the boss had just been brainstorming out loud, not giving directives.

Jokes from the boss don't always go over very well, either, especially when the listener's insecurities imbue them with double and triple meanings. Also, be especially mindful of what you say when approaching a performance review or bonus time. These are times when the possibility of being misinterpreted are greatest, since the people you supervise will be searching for any—and I do mean any—clue of what's to come, resulting in gossip that can spread like wildfire.

If you are confused by the reaction of a subordinate, think back to your most recent conversation and run through these three questions in your mind:

- What did I say?

- What did I mean to say?

- What did they hear?

Joel was an executive in the finance department at a utility company. He was anxious to get together with his boss, Spencer, who had been so tied up for weeks that several of their meetings had been canceled. Joel ran into Spencer's boss in the company cafeteria. While chatting in line, Joel mentioned how he hadn't seen Spencer lately, but was anxious to meet with him. It was a causal comment made in the context of a lighthearted discussion. Later, Spencer's boss repeated the conversation to him, and here's what transpired:

What Spencer's boss said to Spencer: *I ran into Joel at lunch and he said he's very anxious to get together with you.*

What he meant: *I know how busy you've been putting out fires, but please take the time to check in with Joel. For one thing, we could really use those forecasts he's been working on, which I'm sure are ready by now.*

What Spencer heard: *You've got to get this time-management thing under control!*

What Spencer said to Joel: *I hear you're upset that I canceled some of our meetings. I'm sorry. I know we're long overdue, but I've had a crisis situation going on in another area that's been taking priority. Oh, and don't worry about talking to my boss. I'm not one to hold a grudge.* [**Then he patted Joel on the back and walked away.**]

What he meant: *I'm feeling bad and somewhat guilty for not being available lately. Who could blame you for being frustrated.*

What Joel heard: *I'm not so upset that I'm going to fire you, but the thought sure crossed my mind. You really shouldn't have done that.*

Luckily, I was able to talk Joel down from the cliff, so to speak, because I had also worked with Spencer for many years and knew that his remark was part shooting from the hip and part sardonic humor. It's yet another reminder, however, that when you're the boss, you can never be too careful or sensitive about how you say what you say.

TREAT EVERYONE EQUALLY.

Sometimes as people rise within an organization, they become dismissive of anyone lower on the pecking order than they are. But be warned: watching someone on a power trip with those beneath their level is always a turn-off. Be it an assistant, the receptionist, a doorman, the driver, or even a waiter serving you and the client lunch, your words and actions will have a powerful effect at the moment and can also come back to haunt you. People remember who was nice to them, and even more they remember who wasn't. You might be surprised by the big consequences this can have for you down the line.

I can already feel a series of "buts" coming on, as in "But

Peggy, get real. Am I expected to be nice when dealing with incompetents, like . . .

> . . . the tech-support guy who couldn't make sense of what was wrong with my laptop after hours on the phone, causing me to miss a very important deadline?"

> . . . the waiter who screwed up big time when he forgot to put in our table's order and delayed our dinner by half an hour, almost making my client miss the last flight of the day out?"

> . . . those temps that my company continues to hire who can hardly spell, are discourteous, or come in late all of the time?"

As much as laziness and incompetence drive me crazy, I'm sorry, folks, there's a certain level of civility that you just don't stoop below no matter how those around you might act. But this is about far more than just having good manners. Being nasty also speaks volumes about someone's real character. As Holly said, after seeing a potential business partner go off on a waiter over an undercooked steak, "It was a real deal breaker for me. If he did that to the poor waitress, imagine what he might do to the assistant of a potential new client. His hair-trigger behavior could reflect badly on me." And Holly is not alone in her thinking. Research has shown that in both professional and personal situations, being rude to the waiter is perceived as one of the biggest etiquette no-no's of all.

Treating everyone you encounter equally well—regardless of rank—will pay long-term dividends. I'll end the subject by leaving you with a few anecdotes pulled from dozens of stories on how kindness can either pay big returns or leave you smarting.

Tony, well known as someone who treated his support staff

with great respect and appreciation, was in the office of a new client, a major Fortune 500 CEO, waiting for her to arrive so their meeting could begin. Opening his briefcase, he realized to his horror that he had forgotten to bring the entire detailed analysis of her financial portfolio. Just as he was about to have an anxiety attack, his assistant suddenly appeared in the doorway. Realizing Tony had left the presentation on his desk that morning, but unable to reach him because he had turned off his cell phone, she had jumped in a taxi and followed him in hot pursuit across town with the folder in hand.

Tom was in the office one Sunday cramming for a big presentation. Stepping out to grab a quick bite, he realized he had locked himself out and, unfortunately, no one else was at the office that day. He then remembered the janitor, Henry. The two had engaged in friendly conversation throughout the years whenever Tom was working late. Recalling how Henry mentioned that he lived right around the corner, Tom took a chance and Googled the janitor's name on his cell phone. Sure enough, the home phone number popped up. Within minutes of calling, Henry was on his way over to let Tom back in.

Debbie, an entrepreneur in the food world, received an unexpected last-minute call from the producer of a top-rated morning show. It was a Friday night and the producer was looking for a food expert to appear live the following Monday. He thought of Debbie, who had appeared a few times on the local television station ages ago. Back then, the producer was a gofer at the station—the person that rode the elevator up with guests and escorted them to makeup. Now, three years later, the seemingly inconsequential chitchat between the two had resulted in a tremendous business-building opportunity for Debbie with an appearance on a national television show that every high-paid Manhattan publicist would have killed for to land for one of their clients.

Hanna was an administrative assistant to the head of information services, the worst boss she had ever had. Downright moody, demeaning, controlling, and bad tempered, he would be perfectly fine one day and then verbally abusive the next. The final blow came the morning he flipped Hanna off—yes, he gave her "the finger"—as a way to signal "don't interrupt me" when she accidentally walked in his office during a heated telephone discussion with his wife. That was it. She walked out the door and quit.

Within twenty-four hours, the company CEO had caught wind of Hanna's departure and called her to find out what happened. Years ago, they both started out at the company at the same time—she was in the secretarial pool and he was on the management track. Although she had left the workforce for some time to raise her children, Hanna had rejoined the company in the last year and the two were still on friendly terms.

"I'm going to be honest with you, Jake," she told the CEO. "It's been hell to work for this guy." Hanna went on to list a variety of things, ending with the finger story. The CEO was stunned into silence. Then he promised her he was going to "get to the bottom of this," which he did with a quick call to HR. Turns out that several complaints about similar incidents involving Hanna's boss were in his file. Before the afternoon was over, he was fired.

The next day, the CEO called Hanna to apologize for her supervisor's behavior and to ask her to consider taking her job back—reporting, of course, to a new head of information services.

THE IMPOSTOR SYNDROME WILL FOLLOW YOU UP THE LADDER.

While we are on the subject of treating everyone equally, are you including yourself in this equation? It's often easier to believe in others and give them the benefit of doubt than it is to have confidence in ourselves. Here's something else that's likely to pay you many visits during the course of your career—no matter what line of work you are in or how high you climb. By becoming aware of it in yourself, you can work on overcoming it.

Each time you move up a notch, you might hear a little voice in your head that whispers, "Boy, have you pulled a fast one. You really aren't good enough to have this many people counting on you. You don't deserve a job with this much responsibility." Or as a friend who was stepping into a major management position, recently told me, "Peggy, I feel like such an impostor." I replied, "Of course you do, and you probably will until you learn how to play the new role."

Many of us seem to suffer from this same problem—thankfully, not all at the same time—of feeling that we are bluffing our way through the job and hoping that no one will find us out. Referred to as the impostor syndrome, it leaves us fearful of being exposed as mere mortals shaking in our boots, much like the Wizard of Oz when Toto pulled back the curtain. Although I've observed this anxiety in numerous men and women, especially managers, women seem to be far more vocal about expressing it.

Such was the case with one of my clients who was recently offered a much larger job within her organization. When she called in a panic over what to do, I couldn't believe my ears, because she was on the verge of not taking the position.

"But I'm really concerned, Peggy, because I've never done this before," she said.

I reminded her that she had never before done the job she was in at the moment, either. But here she was—four years into it—receiving kudos and being asked to step into a more senior position. This still didn't reassure her, so I took another approach and asked what she had done to learn her current job.

"I pulled it out of my you-know-what. That's what I did!" she shot back, as if possessed.

I laughed hearing her repeat one of my own irreverent expressions that I'd used on her during our coaching sessions, then responded with a challenge: "Well, that's partially true, but I know there was a lot more involved. I want you to think about all of the things you've done to be able to perform so well in your current job."

The next morning, she called back and said, "Last night, I made my list, and you know, I can handle the new position. I'll just need to take all the skills and experiences from my other jobs, learn a few more tricks, and that should do it." Badda bing. Now she had it.

The surest way to beat the impostor syndrome is to act as if you are both competent and confident, even if you don't have all your Is dotted and Ts crossed. I often tell people who think they belong at the next level to start acting like someone who is already there. As an executive at one of my recent workshops explained, she divides businesspeople into three camps: the competents, the confidents, and those with both qualities. Some people are competent but have little or no confidence, others are confident despite little or no competence (these folks are less likely to suffer from the impostor syndrome!)—but the winners are those who learn to marry confidence with competence, a rare combination.

Which brings me to my final point. On one hand, feeling like an impostor isn't always a bad thing, since it drives you to constantly improve yourself and to excel—qualities that great leaders possess. Having said that, you have to be really careful that you don't go overboard in questioning yourself and your abilities, to the point of becoming so frenetic and fearful that you fall short of that winning, "double C" combination.

A LITTLE HUMILITY TAKES YOU A LONG WAY.

Forty-two-year-old Jean was a great manager, or so she thought until her team spun out of control. I met her at a conference when she approached me at the end of the session to introduce herself. I had some unscheduled time before my next event, and so, over a cup of coffee, Jean shared the story of what had compelled her to attend my workshop that day on managing difficult people.

Jean was a senior editor at a major metropolitan daily who currently supervised a team of five department heads. During fifteen years in the newspaper business, she had been given increasingly more management responsibility and had excelled with ease. She credited her success to hard work, intelligence, and her years as an award-winning journalist. "After all," Jean told me, "I never had formal management training and don't read up on the subject much." She thought she had just stumbled into something she was naturally good at.

The past year, however, Jean's picture-perfect world started crumbling around her. The decline began when one of the copy editors complained about the quality of stories she was receiving. As Jean relayed, "My copy editor said, 'I'm here for spelling and grammar, but this stuff is simply unreadable.'" The stories were coming out of a department headed by Marla, who was a fairly recent hire. Despite Jean's attempts to address the issue with her, the problems persisted to the point where the copy editor threatened to refuse to touch anything that Marla submitted. The conflict was getting out of hand, with the other department editors taking sides in the matter. Suddenly, to her extreme embarrassment, Jean's happy newspaper family had dissolved into total dysfunction.

Then, as she explained, Jean had a revelation. It hit her that what was happening at work was similar to her experience as a parent years ago. "When I had my first two children, I thought I was the best mom in the world. They ate well and slept well. On days when the weather forced them inside all day, they would sit quietly and do puzzles. Even my mom's house with its fragile tchotchkies galore required no childproofing before they came over. Grandma would tell the kids, 'Don't touch,' and they didn't. I was smugly convinced that my incredible mothering skills were the reason I had two of the most well-behaved children in the world." When Jean saw other kids running wild, heard stories of them waking up at all hours of the night, or watched them whining and squirming at the dinner table, she thought all the other mommies had to be doing something wrong. That was until she had her third baby. "This one was totally high maintenance from the get-go," Jean told me. "She knocked over my mom's favorite lamp, shattering it into a million pieces, acted so badly at the supermarket that I stopped taking her with me to avoid getting 'the look' from other shoppers, and didn't sleep through the night for her first three years. I couldn't control her at home or in public. With my third, after thinking I was such a hotshot parent with the first two, I simply had no idea what I was doing."

Once Jean realized that she had been blessed with naturally easy-to-manage kids the first two times, she started seeking help with her third—talking to the pediatrician, asking other moms for advice, reading child-rearing books, and attending parenting classes. And once Jean connected the similarities of her mom experience with her work situation, she quickly was able to identify the problem and solution. "I saw that my initial success as a manager wasn't so much about my fabulous abilities, but rather that I'd had the good fortune of having people on my teams with great chemistry and no major shortcomings."

Now it was time for Jean to roll up her sleeves and add some serious new skills to her bag of tricks, which was what prompted her to attend the conference and my session. As she said, "Being an effective manager requires the humility to admit that it's time to go back to being a learner again."

I couldn't have said it any better myself. Well, actually, I would add one more thing, which is this: Continuing to learn and improve yourself isn't just good advice for managers. It's good advice for everyone. No matter where you are in your career, whether just starting out or well on your way, you're always a work in progress.

Afterword

DON'T SKIP YOUR SOFT SKILLS

The best and the brightest—lawyers, doctors, mechanical engineers, educators, investment bankers, journalists, and people with PhD's in fields I can't even pronounce—have told me that soft skills are the hardest thing they've ever had to learn. But here's the good news. They didn't have this book to help them, and you do! You now have the soft skills wisdom, tools, and techniques you'll need to navigate and succeed at work in any situation.

Mastering soft skills takes persistence. It requires that you be mindful about yourself and your career. It demands that you look honestly and critically at your behavior, as well as genuinely being open to feedback—whether good or bad. Mastering these practical and tactical skills doesn't magically happen over night. It requires hard work, but the payoff can be tremendous.

Calling soft skills "soft" is an oxymoron. There's nothing soft about a promising career failing to launch, stalling, or derailing. There's not an ounce of warmth or fuzziness in any of that—in fact, those scenarios can be downright cold and clammy. So whether you are an extroverted marketing person or an introverted engineer, mastering the soft skills will serve you well. And since you've read this book, don't let me catch you repeating what so many of my clients have asked me in the past, "Peggy, why didn't someone tell me . . . ?" Because now I have!

SHARE YOUR STORIES

We would love to hear about your successes and struggles using the soft skills lessons in this book. For details on submitting your stories and for updated information about *The Hard Truth About Soft Skills,* please visit the author's Web site at www.peggyklaus. com.

BRING *THE HARD TRUTH ABOUT SOFT SKILLS* TO YOUR NEXT EVENT OR TRAINING PROGRAM

Peggy Klaus is available as a keynote speaker, corporate trainer, and executive coach on a variety of soft skills topics. For details on her communication and leadership services for groups or individuals, please visit www.peggyklaus.com, e-mail info@peggyklaus.com, or call 510-464-5921.

ACKNOWLEDGMENTS

Although I am not someone who generally feels compelled to express myself in the written form—to spend hours laboring over syntax or searching for the right word—a passion for sharing workplace lessons has turned me into an author yet again. Fortunately, I've had two brilliant collaborators on this project: Jane Rohman and Molly Hamaker. Their extraordinary insight and creativity, not to mention good-natured persistence, has been invaluable in bringing this book to life. Genoveva Llosa was the perfect editor, wielding her mighty pen with a loving heart. Much gratitude goes to Sarah Brown for her many contributions during the final stages of this project. Of course, I wouldn't have had the pleasure of working with them had it not been for my agent, Jim Levine. A special thanks also to my associate Sarah Rees, who somehow manages to keep both me and my business going with grace and a great sense of humor. Last, but always first in my heart, my appreciation and love to Randy, who continues to support, challenge, and amaze me.

INDEX

ABOUT THE AUTHOR

PEGGY KLAUS has spent more than a decade as a communication and leadership coach advising top Fortune 500 executives and employees. President of Klaus & Associates, based in Berkeley, California, she reaches thousands of professionals worldwide each year through her speaking, coaching, and workshops at leading companies, including JPMorgan Chase, Levi Strauss, American Express, Disney, Goldman Sachs, Cisco Systems, and Booz Allen Hamilton, among many others. Klaus is also the author of *BRAG! The Art of Tooting Your Own Horn Without Blowing It.* Her colorful and frank advice is frequently sought out by journalists and she has been featured extensively in a wide range of media, including ABC's *20/20,* NBC's *Today, BusinessWeek,* the *Wall Street Journal,* the *New York Times, Newsweek, Fortune,* and *O* magazine.

Well regarded in higher education, Klaus has lectured on communication to students and faculty at the University of California, Berkeley's Haas School of Business, School of Law, and School of Public Health. She has also served as lecturer at Wharton's Executive MBA program, the Pepperdine University School of Law, and Harvard's John F. Kennedy School of Government. Additionally, she sits on the Kennedy School of Government's Women's Leadership Board. When not teaching or training people how to communicate and lead, Klaus can be found at Lost Canyon Winery in Oakland, California, which she co-owns with her husband.